THE MYSTERY 0F CHRIST IN YOU

© Copyright 2010

By Earl W. Lacy

All Rights reserved

ISBN 13:   978-0-9970856-7-9
ISBN 10:   0997085673

Ecclesia Publishing House LLC
United States of America
ecclesiaph@gmail.com

Table of Contents

Page

CHAPTER ONE   THE MYSTERY   3

The Seed

CHAPTER TWO   FROM DEATH TO LIFE   25

Weep Not!

CHAPTER THREE   THE WORD WAS MADE FLESH   49

The Mystery Of Christ

All Men Seek For Thee

The Lamb For Sinners Slain

CHAPTER FOUR   JESUS IS ALIVE   90

Awesome Spirit Being

CHAPTER FIVE   PRAYER, PRAISE AND WORSHIP   113

God Is Spirit

The Resurrection Covenants

CHAPTER SIX   SERPENTS IN OUR GARDEN   154

New Wineskins

Raising Lazarus

I Am Determined!

CHAPTER ONE
THE MYSTERY

[For my determined purpose is] that I may know Him"
Phil.3.10 (Amp. Bible).

All is utterly and eternally worthless compared to knowing Christ. This was the conclusion of the matter as far as the Apostle Paul, formally Saul of Tarsus was concerned.

The old Saul was an enemy to himself and of Christ; he was a religious man motivated by pride, embracing corruption. Once he sold his soul and swore loyalty to the peddlers of the wisdom of this world; Gamaliel was Saul's teacher, who taught Saul that the ways of the Pharisees were the ways of God.

Saul's determined purpose was to please those whom pleased God. Having letters from the Sanhedrin Council, the Jewish Supreme Court to arrest the disciples of Jesus of Nazareth—Christians, he brought them bound in chains to Jerusalem to stand trial, or rather, a religious lynch mob.

But on the road to Damascus, Syria, Saul had a life-changing encounter with the Lord Jesus Christ. Saul was transformed from a Hell-bound Anointing-less sinner into a man endowed with the yoke-destroying, burden-lifting, devil-stomping Resurrection Anointing; he became a saint of the New Testament Covenant!

From his first encounter with the Lord, Saul, now given the name of Paul, purposed in his heart to know the Lord Jesus. This "knowing" wasn't limited to mere knowledge, but to actually Know, Love, Praise and Worship, to trust in His Person as the source of his Eternal Life; to know Jesus Christ, as his "personal" Lord and Savior.

Everything he had accomplished was but a shadow compared to the Light of Christ. All the confidence he had in the flesh was gone; all his personal achievements---all gains became but lost compared to knowing Him, and was counted as dung. This revelation came to him as the indwelling Christ made Himself known to Paul's spirit and soul. Christ revealed the Mystery and the Resurrection Anointing.

As Christ the Wisdom of God unveiled the Mystery and the Resurrection Anointing to Paul, He desires to do the same in His Church.

Therefore, our determined purpose must be to know Christ better. We must seek to be intimately acquainted with Him. Through diligently studying the Holy Bible and seeking divine revelation from Christ within our spirit, we can receive and perceive by divine intuition, know and understand the greatness of His Person, and be conformed to His image; we can experience His daily Life and the out-flow from His resurrection and the fullness of the Anointing which exerts and changes us while still in the physical body.

There's also a price to pay to knowing the Lord Jesus Christ; we must also experience and share His sufferings and death by crucifixion. Without the death of the self-life there can be no resurrection. In order that deep can call unto deep, the Anointing must exert Himself over the life and affairs of Believers.

As Christ laid hold of Saul--a spiritually dead man---and changed him to Paul, he expressed the hope to lay hold of the One who first loved and took hold of him; we too must have the same hope.

Everyone loves a mystery! In Luke 9:28-31, Jesus took Peter, James and John upon a mountain to pray. There, Jesus was transfigured before them and His countenance was altered.

The glory of Christ within the man Jesus glistened as white as snow. Suddenly, there appeared Moses and Elijah: The Master had need of them.

This was a divine appointment to discuss the Mystery: This Mystery had been hidden before the foundation of the world. It was necessary that Jesus summoned these two Old Testament prophets from their intern in Sheol. They would return to the place of the dead to prepare the way for the Lord's visit.

Naturally, the subject of the conversation was His "decrease," what Jesus would accomplish at Calvary: His death, resurrection, the Anointing released in the Physical Realm to indwell Believers, was what Jesus talked about. The Resurrection Anointing would be the manifestation of the Faith, Hope and Love of all the ancients who believed the Word of God, the promise of Salvation, the resurrection of the dead, and the Messiah, the Anointed One and the Anointing would come and make His Abode in and among us.

> 10 "Of which salvation the prophets have inquired and searched diligently, who prophesied of the grace that should come unto you: 11 Searching what, or what manner of time the Spirit of Christ which was in them did signify, when it testified beforehand the SUFFERINGS OF CHRIST AND THE GLORY THAT SHOULD FOLLOW. 12 ...which things the ANGELS DESIRE TO LOOK INTO" 1 Peter 1:10-12 (King James Version)

The suffering, death, and resurrection of Jesus of Nazareth, the Anointed One and His Salvation wasn't only inquired into by the holy prophets, but the holy angels were interested in understanding (but not being Human, were not eligible to experience) God's Redemption Plan. It's also true that Satan and his principalities were dumbfounded. Their interests, of course, was to derail God's plan and keep Man bound in and because of sin. Yet, the Mystery remained hidden from them, because they lost their first estate in Heaven.

Christ is the Power and Wisdom of God (1 Cor. 1.24). Christ is the Mystery, Who was ordained before the foundation of the world. But none of the princes, the rulers, principalities and powers presiding over this cursed and fallen realm knew, "for had they known it, they would not have crucified the Lord of glory" (1 Cor. 2.8). Therefore, it's not easy but possible to know Christ. He is willing to make Himself known.

Why is it that the demonic authorities couldn't figure out the Mystery? Religious people give too much credit to Satan. He isn't as intelligent or powerful as many believe.

In the Gospel of John 1.4,5 it reads, In Him was life; and the Life was the Light of men, and the Light shines in darkness, and the darkness comprehended it not."

The Light and Life is Christ; His Person and Anointing flows; Satan and his associates cannot comprehend or quench Christ, nor can they even understand, predict or monitor His movements.

The darkness influence upon the un-saved and those whose minds are carnal; all day long, the minds of mankind are flooded with demonic and suggestive images, deceiving spirits blanket them with the same ignorance and deceptions the demonic powers suffer from. Because demons love darkness more than the Light of Christ the Mystery, they want us to love darkness too!

> "Light has come into the world, and people have loved the darkness rather than and more the Light, for their works (deeds) were evil" (John 1:19 Amp.).

The contents of this scripture pertains to the Word becoming flesh; the Word is Christ the Light of the world. Because the darkness and those who are blinded by it cannot appropriate the Light, people love the darkness more and rather than the Light--- because they don't want to change.

Thus, the Sin Indictment, a Verdict and Judgment handed down by God---remains on them, and the Resurrection Anointing cannot raise them in the spirit, soul, and body, because they won't let go of the darkness and accept the Light of Christ.

Unbelief is failure to cleave to, rely on, or trust in Christ; this condemns the soul to be held by chains of darkness, the very chains that hold fallen angels upon the Earth and others in Hell.

That is why we as Christians must pray for and assist in the evangelizing of the world. We MUST assist and intercede for the salvation of the lost, and pray that the chains, the yokes are destroyed because of the Anointing. The Anointing is designed, "To open their eyes, and to turn them from darkness to Light, and from the power of Satan unto God, that they may receive forgiveness of sins, and INHERITANCE among them which are sanctified by faith that is in Me" (Acts 26:13). God can do everything His Word says He can.

The Mystery, hidden from angels and devils alike, is Christ in us. This Mystery was conceived in the heart of God before the foundation of the world. God hinted about it when He spoke of the "Seed" crushing the serpent's head.

God further developed His plan and revealed portions of it to Abraham, David, Isaiah, Daniel and others. It was God's plan that Jesus of Nazareth become the temple of the incarnated Christ, live a sinless life, die the cursed death upon the cross--and be resurrected from the dead by the commandment of God; and thus release the awesome creativity of God, the Resurrection Anointing which also created the Church.

The Holy Spirit (who is also the Lord!) adopts spiritual children into the family of God; He cannot bring those born only of the flesh, but those who are Born of the Spirit. Then Christ is pleased to make known by His Spirit the generosity of the Father of spirits: "To the intent that now unto the [demonic] principalities and powers in the heavenly places might be known BY THE CHURCH the manifold wisdom [Christ, the Wisdom of God]."

The Church expresses the manifold wisdom of God: Christians are the Church at the throne of God and in the Physical Realm. It's our duty to enforce the victory that was won at Calvary. Angels who desire to understand the Anointed One and the Anointing look to the Church to manifest and reveal Him; even demonic spirits are watching the Church in hope of quenching, grieving the Holy Spirit which flows out of our bellies, the rivers of living water empowering us to do supernatural and mighty works--healing the blind, deaf, diseased and raising people from the dead--but demons can't understand the profound message of faith; neither can they break the security of the Word, Name, and the Blood of Jesus--so they bow and flee in terror! Those who aren't redeemed struggle with the Mystery.

THE SEED

The Holy Scriptures declare that, "In the beginning God created the heavens and the earth" (Genesis 1:1). That statement is to inform us that God prepared, formed and fashioned the heavens and the earth out of vacuum space--nothingness. He didn't manipulate things that were tangible--material substances; but His FAITH was the SUBSTANCE of the things He hoped for, the EVIDENCE of the things He conceived in His heart.

In His Faith Heaven, Physical Realm, and Man already existed but was not yet manifested. He made available what was unavailable, and called those things that be not as though they were; He made something out of nothing. Hence, God possesses the ability to create, sustain or resurrect anything or anyone that He chooses.

The Word continued to explain the direct interaction and re-lationship God had and still has with His creation: God SAID let there be light, firmament, waters, plants, heavenly bodies, animals, and lastly—

Man. In Genesis 1:26-28, "God said, Let Us [Father, Son, and Holy Spirit] make mankind in Our image, after Our likeness, and let them have complete AUTHORITY over the fish of the sea..." Complete dominion implies that Man received the delegated authority from God to subdue and use the vast resources of the Holy Spirit and creation to the service of God and the prosperity of mankind; even the heavens declare the glory of God. God approved of Man when He created him in His own image, and after His likeness.

Also, before the foundation of the world God blessed mankind and predestined the Blessing. Through His omniscience, being the Alpha and Omega, the Beginning and the Ending of all things--He knew before He created Adam that Adam would disobey and rebel against His authority, and thus fall from the grace and heavenly dignity.

The Almighty also knew that beloved Adam would forfeit the title deed of ownership to the Physical Realm to Satan. So God heaped up the Blessing, an inheritance of exceedingly great and precious promises, gifts and Anointing to lavishly pour out upon mankind once his obedience is fulfilled.

Included in these promises are Salvation--the resurrection of the spiritually dead human spirit, restoring of the soul and mind, healing and soundness of the physical body, material prosperity, and an exclusive wealthy place and state of heavenly dignity--Man would be an awesome spirit being. The total contents of the package comprises of the Mystery. "And I will put enmity between you and the woman, and between your seed and her Seed; it shall bruise your head, and you shall bruise His heel" (Genesis 3:15). God's plan wasn't in response to Satan's deception in the Garden of Eden, but in response to His original plan for restoring mankind after the fall.

God cursed Satan and drew a line-in-the-sand separating Satan's children from His own. He thus implemented His original plan to win back the Physical Realm and its lordship from Satan and present it into the hands of His Seed. Then the Lord Jesus Christ, the Administrator of the Blessing will present it to the Church.

God predestinated that the Seed "planted" in the womb of the Virgin Mary, the mother of Jesus would be the Word, the Revelation of God made flesh. He would crush the serpent's head, take Satan's authority over death and rule the Physical Realm in Covenant with the Saints.

God wasn't caught asleep or on vacation. He swore with an oath to every living creature that He wouldn't fail: "DECLARING THE END FROM THE BEGINNING, and from ancient times, the things that are not yet done, saying, My counsel shall stand, and I will do all My pleasure" (Isa. 46:10).

So you see, Jesus of Nazareth crucified wasn't God's backup plan to save face with the holy angels or the Devil, but was His original plan before He created Adam.

God didn't cancel His vision for a human family to praise and worship Him, because He knew in advance that Lucifer would corrupt Adam; He included the solution to the perceived problem; and in the Spirit Realm, the Lamb was slain before God created Adam.

It's good to know that God chose and handpicked us for Himself. Through the Adoption Agency of the Holy Spirit, He loved us so much that He wants to reveal Himself as Christ within us. This pleases Him and has always been His ultimate goal and kind intent: To be a Father and have lovely, spiritual children.

He chose us because it pleased Him. God has a plan for our lives and this plan doesn't include the wages of sin which amounts to death. The plan does include an Anointed and blessed life, unless we prefer our own plans and paths over His. It's up to us if we want to be a sin-slaves or righteous-servants. Whatever pleases God ought to please us too.

What is Man that God is so concerned about him? We're a little lower than Elohim (God), made in His image and likeness and joint-heirs---something that not even the holy angels can claim as their own. We're entitled to bask in the glory of God.

Because In Christ are the treasures of wisdom, purpose and spiritual knowledge; those treasures that were once hidden but are now revealed and being administered by Jesus Christ, the Messiah, the Anointed One.

Christ is the center and focal point of everything God has planned for us; there's nothing outside of Christ that God is remotely interested in. Only what is initiated or approved by the Son of God survives the fire. Christ is God's hidden treasure; Christ is His wisdom, power, delight, reflection and the brightness of His glory.

Receiving Christ in us, we assimilate the wealth of comprehensive insight into His ways and purposes. We also receive mental, physical and material prosperity which translates into "nothing missing, nothing broken."

We have assurance from God that He's a partner in our Salvation. We are joint-heirs with Jesus Christ; everything He is in righteousness and truth, we too are the righteousness of God in Christ. All that He has won in victory over Satan, we share in the treasures of His inheritance; and, we are also considered His inheritance, part of what He accomplished at Calvary, in bringing many sons into glory.

He will cause everything to work together for our good because He is mighty and able to make it so. Everything, the good, the bad, and the ugly---works together for our good and the counsel of His will---is fitting into His eternal plan, his design and purpose for the ages and dispensations to come.

Because God knew us before He formed us in the womb, even before the world began, He has a plan for our lives; He molds and shapes us to be all that we can be In Him. He does this from the inside out, in order that we share an inward likeness and personality like Jesus Christ, the Anointed One.

God also acquitted us of the crime of sin and placed us in right standing with Himself, and seated together with Him at the Throne of God, in a state of heavenly grace and dignity.

This should be shouting material! The paths of God include His guidance. We cannot embark upon this spiritual journey without a guide. We're a spirit being journeying in the Physical Realm; we're not a physical being having a spiritual experience!

As soon as we acknowledge the truth down in our heart, the sooner we can be on the way to victory and taking dominion over ourselves and the environment. Denial will only lead us deeper into darkness. The Holy Spirit is our Guide.

The purpose of the Resurrection Anointing is to recreate us, renew our Human spirit and restore the soul which constitutes the mental facilities of intellect, emotions, will, and imagination (creativity). In the end

It also leads to complete glorification of our physical body, but presently overcoming sickness and disease. The last enemy is physical death; it is swallowed up in victory!

Everything God has done is because He loves us; everything He predestined is because it's best for us. We're the fruit of His labor of love in the vineyard, the manifestation of centuries of His Spirit pressing His way through the darkness of human history, to manifest the Light of the World.

He fought off numerous attacks by the meanest Devil, and now is entitled to enjoy the fruits of His vineyard. And because God planned this beforehand, we too can enjoy the fruits of predestined paths that He chose for us to walk in.

Oh, what love the Father has for us! He has prearranged divine paths for us to walk in and live the abundant life. On these paths His Anointing awaits to fall upon us and empower us to do great and mighty deeds for the Kingdom.

Everything we need to reach spiritual maturity awaits us; the Resurrection Anointing is Elohim-Life.

God prepared assignments for us: We transport the Holy Spirit in our earthen vessel to the proper destination, and He will do the work. Every assignment on the paths are initiated by Him so the fruit will survive His judgment.

These works are not of the Tree of the Knowledge of Good and Evil, blessings or calamity, where festers rebellion, self-centeredness and self-gratification, but the fruits of God are from the Tree of Life, Himself. These paths and works are holy manifestations of the counsel of His will.

David said, "The Lord is my Shepherd, I shall not want" (Ps. 23.1). David was himself a shepherd, before he was Anointed King of Israel and was mighty to slay Goliath.

The Good Shepherd is our all-seeing and perfect guide as we travel through this dark, sin-cursed and demon-infested world, where abides the valley of the shadow of death. We will be taken care of, our needs will be supplied according to God's heavenly economy

His glory is the awesome weight of excellence and goodness. We shall be protected and lack nothing; no good thing shall be withheld from us by our Heavenly and all-wise Father. His Spirit shall restore our entire being, and give us the inward likeness, integrity, the Fruit of the Spirit. He will counsel and comfort us in times of adversity, strengthen us with might by the power of His Spirit within our innermost being, so that Christ may dwell in our heart through increased faith. Indeed, the Blessing will come upon us and overtake us!

The table He prepares for us provides more than we can use, so we can sow financial seeds into the lives and ministries of others. God grants this abundant surplus from His storehouses throughout the earth.

Our neighbors call us blessed--happy and to be envied--because the Lord is so good to us; but the Devil complains to God that we're pampered with material things, and, like he said of Job, if this prosperity were taken we would curse God to His face. Yet, it's the Father's good pleasure to give us the Kingdom, and it's our love and faith that motivates us to Praise and Worship our Lord; the gifts are only benefits.

The Anointing upon us heals the sick, casts out demons and raises people from the dead. Our heads, anointed with the oil of the Holy Spirit, runs over like lava flowing down a volcano---flowing with goodness, mercy and unfailing love, the unmistakable Presence of Christ in us, touching our mortal life and the lives of others. We shall abide in the state of bliss and heavenly dignity forever.

> "Now the LORD had said to Abraham, Get thee out of thy country, and from thy kindred, and from thy father's house, unto a land that I will show thee. And I will make of thee a great nation, and I will bless thee, and make thy name great; and thou shall be a blessing" (Genesis 12:1,2).

The divine providence of God reached into the Physical Realm and He called upon Abram. God contacted a man He could communicate His plan to. Abram moved with reverence at the hearing of the voice of Almighty God. He obeyed, and God counted it as righteousness.

When God called Abram he was a heathen and an idol worshipper. He was the offspring of a long line of sinners. Nevertheless, God spoke to Abram's heart, the inner man, and activated the measure of faith which every human being has. The first thing God told Abraham was, "wherefore, come out from among them and be ye separate, says the Lord..." (2 Corinthians 6:17).

God commanded, not suggested, that he distance himself from

the world and its passions, so that He could establish Covenant with him. Relatives often get in the way when a Believer attempts to be obedient and serve God.

God would bless Abram and he would be a blessing; through him it was possible for Abram to save his father and nations of kindred. Through Abram the entire world would be blessed because of his Obedience to God. The time had come for God to establish the great genealogical line of descendents to bring forth the Promised Seed. The Seed, Jesus of Nazareth, would crush Satan's head.

God called and separated Abram from his kindred; God called and separated us from the world and its influences; the problem is, we madly embrace what God has separated us from--and this is why we're struggling with sin. God separated us to sanctify us from the distract-ions and temptations of the self-life for His divine service.

God separated us from the unbelievers, doubters, hypocrites, religions and traditions of men, because they make the Word of God of no effect: They are the enemies of faith. This separation is the same as God commanded in the Garden of Eden: The separation of His own Seed from the seed of the Wicked One.

> "And when Abram was ninety years old and nine, the LORD appeared to Abram, and said unto him, I am the Lord God, walk before Me, and be thou perfect. And I will establish My Covenant between me and thy Seed after thee in their generations for an everlasting covenant, to be a God unto thee, and to thy Seed forever" (Genesis 17:1,7).

That day Abram's name was changed to Abraham. He became a new creature with a Covenant. For decades God dealt with Abram, that old heathen idol-worshipping sinner, to give birth in his soul the revelation of who God is, and His plans, purposes and pursuits in the Physical Realm; plus the revelation of who Abram was as a servant of God, and what the name "Abraham" meant. The revelation had to get down in Abram's inner man. By faith he had to "see" himself as blessed, and every time he said his own name, he declared: Father of many nations--only then could it come to pass in the natural. It wasn't until this day that Abram was delivered from his "demons" and could be used of God.

Through the obedience of the new creature--Abraham, God made an agreement, a blood Covenant with a free moral agent residing in the Physical Realm. God channeled His authority to Covenant.

The Human seed would bring forth the Divine Seed; this in itself constitutes a mystery. Isaac was the descendent of Abraham chosen of God to bring forth the Seed. God wasn't in a hurry; He never rushes into anything.

Years later God tested the obedience and faith of Abraham. God told Abraham to prepare Isaac as a burnt offering. Abraham moved quickly. He knew the God he served was holy and would accept nothing less than compliance. The revelation of God remained strong in Abraham's soul. He knew in whom he had believed: God wouldn't break His Word and take his son, the heir of the Promise.

Being a prophet, Abraham also received revelation of the resurrection of the dead. He knew that God was Life. If God required him to sacrifice Isaac, was because He would raise Isaac from the dead. "And Abraham said, My son, God will provide (Jehovah-Jireh) Himself a lamb for a burnt offering."

Isaac also displayed a monumental faith in God. Isaac was a healthy teenager when the Word of the Lord came to Abraham. Abraham was nearly a hundred years old. Isaac could have gotten free from his father and ran for his life!

Isaac believed that Abraham hadn't gone insane but was obeying the voice of God. So Isaac presented himself as a living sacrifice, a type of Christ, which was his "reasonable service."

> 10 "And Abraham stretched forth his hand, and took the knife to slay his son" Genesis 22:10-13,16,17 (KJV).

We will never be asked to sacrifice one of our children to God because the only sacrifice that was acceptable to God was Jesus Christ. Yet the purpose of the test is whether we love God more than everything else; to love God *is* the first, greatest and most weighty of the Commandments.

We most certainly will be asked to give up the usual suspects: Alcohol, drugs, sexual sins, stealing, criminal activities, cursing, lying, and several toxic friendships.

But most of us don't think about Halloween, detestable objects such as certain paintings and statues; and we think even less about toxic relationships, soul tie friends (sex partners), associations and lodges such as the Eastern Star Free Masons, fraternities and sororities (because of sworn oaths), bars, sometimes motor cycle clubs, hangouts and other places and things that are near to our heart but detrimental to our spiritual growth.

The things we give up are things associated with the kingdom of darkness, things that hinder our spiritual growth. These things are like tentacles with suckers that wrap around us and pull us into the jaws of destruction.

The call to obedience keeps our focus on the Lord and away from the world. The love of the world is enmity to God. We're not to love the World System. This love of the soul life, the self separates us from God, Who, would have everyone be saved and come to the knowledge of the truth. The self-life is an infatuation with mortality, at the expense of immortality,

In God's wisdom Abraham wasn't a perfect but a complete man. When God tested him the test was based on the revelation knowledge imparted to him; his compliance was based on his personal relationship with God. His faith in God wasn't based on hearsay or family tradition, or what his friends thought.

The New Testament writers informed us the Promise that Abraham would be the heir of the world wasn't to him, or his genealogical off-spring, but to those who are the spiritual children of the Seed (Romans 4:13 9:8).

This assures us that we're included in the Promise. "Even as Abraham believed God, and it was accounted to him as right-eousness" (Galatians 3:6), our heavenly bank accounts grow plump as we put our trust in God who cannot lie. He honors faith as substance acceptable to Him as sacrifice and fruit of our lips giving praises unto His glorious Name. There is one Blessing, also known as the Promise; this Blessing includes numerous promises and benefits. There is one Seed, for all the spiritual heirs are seeds and in Him; Christ gives birth to spiritual children.

The Apostle Paul wrote to some extent on this subject, confirming to the Gentiles, who didn't know God, the certainty and inclusive nature of His Promise.

"Now the promise (covenants, agreements) were decreed and

made to Abraham and his Seed (his Offspring, his heir). He (God) does not say, and to seeds (descendants, heirs), as in referring to many persons, but, And to your Seed (your descendents, heirs), obviously referring to one individual, Who is [none other than] Christ (the Messiah)."

In Hebrews 6:13,17, it's written: "For God made promise to Abraham, because He could swear by no greater, He swore by Himself...Wherein God, willing more abundantly to show unto the heirs of promise the immutability (unchangeableness) of His counsel, confirmed it by an oath: That by two immutable things, in which it was IMPOSSIBLE FOR GOD TO LIE, we might have a strong consolation who fled for refuge to lay hold upon the hope set before us."

God's Word as an oath was the hope that anchored the soul of Abraham. Without this anchor, like a ship in port, could easily be blown out to sea during a violent storm---Abraham had nowhere promising to direct his Faith. Without the Promise and the oath from God who cannot lie, we may easily stumble, waver in our faith and fall. The Holy Spirit has revealed to our spirit the certainty of the resurrection.

By Faith we adhere to, trust in, and rely on Christ who quickens the dead, and calls those things that be not as though they were. God was the refuge and strength of the Old Testament saints.

Throughout the ages, God has glorified and magnified His Name in the Physical Realm. He has left a reputation in keeping His Word.

Notes

CHAPTER TWO
FROM DEATH TO LIFE

Adam disobeyed God so sin entered him and all his descendants were automatically born in sin and iniquity. But in the same way that one man's transgression many were made sinners, how much more fitting should one Man's right-standing with God deliver us from Adamite sin.

We have become kings and priests because in the same manner that Christ reigns in life we reign with Him.

Death. Even the word sounds terrible, final, abrupt and inescapable. Most of us don't want to think or talk about death. Yet, without the revelation of death, the "fear of death" will undermine everything you do; your decisions will be based upon the risk or fear of death, rather than the joys of living.

Without occasionally pondering death, we cannot know what Christ has freed us from; we cannot appreciate His magnificent Person and the power emanating from His Resurrection.

Without the revelation of the resurrection we cannot personally and intimately know the Lord Jesus Christ and be a conscious participant in His plan; we fall short of the personal relationship we seek.

Death wasn't part of God's plan for Man; death was added to our experience because of Adam's disobedience. When God told Adam, "Thou shall not..." and Adam did, he became a trespasser of the Commandment of God; to break one Commandment was equal to breaking them all. It didn't matter whether God told Adam not to cross a bridge or ride a particular animal, it amounted to rebellion.

To God rebellion is practicing the psychic art of witchcraft; it's the practice of relying on and manifesting the powers of the soul life, the mental powers; it's not walking in the Spirit, but using manipulation, intimidation, and domination. Rebellion is rooted in the Tree of the Knowledge of Good and Evil.

God told Adam not to eat of the forbidden fruit or he would

die; Adam knew that God cannot lie. The wages of his sin became death. The first death he suffered was of his human spirit; the glory of the lord departed like a winged cherub, as it went back to heaven. He lost the Holy Spirit which made him the god of the Physical Realm.

Then came the decline of the soul, the mind operating without the supervision of the Spirit; sinful thoughts and actions resulted. Adam was separated from the divine source of righteousness and influence, as the nature of the Tree of the Knowledge assimilated, took over his mind, and resistance became futile.

He freely entered into the transgression; it wasn't as though Lucifer or something attacked him. But after he had eaten of the Tree Knowledge, he wasn't permitted to eat of the Tree of Life. God wouldn't allow Adam and his descendents to become superhuman criminals who would never die. The Old Testament states: "For the wages of sin is death;" New Testament: "But the gift of God is eternal life through Jesus Christ our Lord" (Romans 6:23). Old Testament: "For since by Man came death." New Testament: "By Man came also the resurrection of the dead" (1 Corinthians 15:21).

Sometimes we need a miracle in our life. A miracle would bring us the love, joy, peace, healing, or the supernatural intervention we need to survive and thrive another day. Facing our own death or the death of a loved one is such a crisis. We need help and we need it now!

From the time of Adam to the arrival of Jesus Christ, millions of people had died. This being so, few have returned from the dead. In First Kings Chapter Seventeen, God sent the Prophet Elijah to a poor widow who lived in Zidon. There was a drought in Israel; the curses written in Deuteronomy Chapter Twenty-Eight were activated by Israel's disobedience.

When Elijah came to the woman. He asked her for a drink of water, then for some bread to eat. This was her pitiful reply: "And she said, As the Lord thy God lives, I have not a cake, but a handful of meal in a barrel, and a little oil in a cruse: and, behold, I am gathering two sticks that I may go and dress it for me and my son, that we may eat it, and die" (v.12).

In the natural, all her hope of continuing in this realm and the life of her son was dried up like the parched ground in Israel. She was as good as dead; the barrel of meal was as good as gone; the oil to mix it would follow suit. She envisioned her family extinction.

Her husband was already dead and shortly she and her son would see him in that mysterious place called Sheol. Yet, before her stood a man who she perceived was a Worshipper of the Lord God of Israel. Why was he here---to bring to remembrance her sins? To declare her punishment here on Earth and not wait to the afterlife?

Or, who was she that this honor should come to her, when kings had messengers roaming throughout the country looking for a real prophet with the Word of the Lord concerning the famine? And why had he appeared only days prior to her starvation? But her immediate concern was: Why did he want her last food?

Elijah comforted her, "Fear not". Of course, that was easy for him to say since the Lord was taking care of him; she was not a Jew and had no covenant relationship. She was afraid. She had come to the end of herself. But something within her said, Have faith and obey. Now she wanted to be a blessing even if it shortened her life. She figured, What difference does it make if she died on Monday instead of Wednesday of the same week?

At his word, the widow made a little cake, then she *made* herself and son a *cake* with the rest. She sowed this tiny seed into the ministry of Elijah; the offering was a faith seed, an unselfish trust in the integrity of the God Elijah served. She knew there were many false prophets with false ministries serving false gods in Israel and in Zidon. Nevertheless, her soul cried out to God and she believed that she was doing the right thing. Her faith seed was sown unto the Lord who judges the living and the dead. The same Lord she knew could even raise the dead.

Elijah declared: "The barrel of meal shall not waste, neither shall the cruse of oil fail, until the day that the LORD sends rain upon the earth" (v.14). The barrel of meal and the oil lasted three long, dry years!

One day her son got sick and died. She was devastated. How could such a thing happen? First her husband died and the income that he brought into the home was lost. Then she and her son almost starved to death. If it had not been for the Grace of God who sent Elijah, they would have been long dead

Satan attacked her with doubt and unbelief; but she knew that her son would stay dead if she listened to him; the Spirit of Death, fear and mayhem had never given her good advice before!

> "Then they that feared the LORD spoke often one to another; and the LORD hearkened, and heard it, and a book of remembrance was written..." Mal. 3:16 (KJV)

Saving the widow and her son wasn't enough for the Lord God of Israel. The widow's faith contacted Him as He sat upon the throne and ruled His kingdom. The Lord remembered her name when He read his Book of Remembrance. Something that the Lord documented the extraordinary Faith, Obedience and Giving of his beloved children who are blessing others. Her faith came up for a memorial. The death of her son also touched His heart.

Elijah perceived her despair. "And he said unto her, Give me thy son" (v.19). She perceived in her soul as though God Himself said, Give Me thy son! So she gave the Lord her son, her only son, and sowed him as a seed offering into the kingdom of God.

> "...0 my LORD, I pray Thee, let this child's soul come into him again. And the LORD heard the voice of Elijah; and the soul of the child came into him again, and he revived" (V.21,22). "And the woman said to Elijah, Now by this I know that thou art a man of God, and that the Word of the LORD in thy mouth is truth" (V.24).

Talk is cheap; this woman needed action, and she needed it right away. Now *she* knew that Elijah was an awesome spirit being with a personal relationship with God, because God manifested through him His awesome Resurrection Anointing. This great power took the sting out of death and brought a sweat-less victory, the type that only God can bring.

The victory was clear and decisive; there was no doubt or disbelief left in the widow that the Lord loved her and her son; and Elijah was an authentic servant who spoke the truth, the whole truth, and nothing but the truth.

Even today God is looking for us to bring down the fire of the Holy Spirit, and stand in the gap between Him and humanity. The Elijahs of the world are few; Elijahs aren't religious people whose relationship is only with the local church or denomination, whose love is only for those who agree with a certain doctrine; Elijahs are those willing to allow God to channel His Resurrection Anointing to destroy yokes of oppression, obsession, and possession. These men and women dedicate themselves to destroy the works of the Devil!

The harvest of souls is plenteous; if we don't harvest the Divine Crop they will rot in Hell. Laborers are needed. God needs maximum exposure in this realm to reach the lost. He's not hiding; but He's a Spirit desiring to make Himself known and felt in the Physical Realm.

Therefore, He's looking to make Christians out of everyone, men and women who will submit to Him and be used in a supernatural way. He's not enlisting an army of religious folks; for religion is the works of Satan.

God needs brave warriors to fight the good fight of faith and lay hold of the Blessing, the Inheritance prepared and made available to us before the foundation of the world. Consistent with redeemed life is the preaching and teaching of the Word; then miracles, signs and wonders will follow. We who are Born Again by the Spirit of God must live like the Spirit of God.

At the end of his ministry, Elijah found his replacement, Elisha. Elijah asked Elisha what could he do for him before he left. Elisha asked for a double portion of his power.

Elijah was taken up by a whirlwind. Elisha saw a chariot and horses of fire take his master. Elijah threw his mantle to Elisha.

Elisha went to Jordan River. "And he took the mantle of Elijah that fell from him, and smote the waters, and said, Where is the LORD God of Elijah? And when he had also smitten the waters, they parted hither and thither: and Elisha went over. And when the sons of the prophets which were to view Jericho saw him, they said, The Spirit of Elijah doth rest upon Elisha. And they came to meet him, and bowed themselves to the ground before him" (2 Kings 2:14,15).

Again the well of Faith overflowed into the Physical Realm and the Anointing came upon Elisha. It was obvious to the sons of the prophets that the Life of God flowed through him in order to manifest the will of God; it was obvious that the Abrahamic Covenant and personal relationship Elijah possessed was now the possession of his successor, and God would do mighty works.

The predestined paths of God brought Elisha to the Shunamitte woman, who had great material wealth. The Word states that she was rich, but she wasn't in love with her wealth. In fact, every time Elisha was in the area she compelled him to come into her home for meals and rest. She realized that it was God who gave her the ability to get wealth; she realized what a blessing she could be in advancing the kingdom of God.

She consulted her husband, who was the head of the house, to build an addition on the house. She had a door cut into the wall, built a room, put in a bed, table, candlestick, and stool in the room. This extra room was specifically built for the prophet. Her determined purpose was to sow a seed into the kingdom of God. She would help God's prophet evangelize the nations; she would show hospitality and provide Elisha shelter, food and personal hygiene while he was away from home. She had no hidden agenda.

Yet God wouldn't allow the Shunammite woman to be more generous than Himself. She had unknowingly touched a tender spot in His personality; she sown a seed at His Throne that had to be reaped. The Book of Remembrance was before Him: The Word went forth to bless the Shunammite woman.

Elisha was also prompted by the Spirit of God. "And he said to Gehazi, his servant, call this Shunammite woman. And when he had called her, she stood before him" (2 Kings 4:12), in the room she had sowed into the kingdom. She had taken so good care of both men that the prophet was ashamed not to ask what could be done for her. Elisha had influence with the king and officials; but he soon discovered that she had influence too. In short, she didn't need his help, and left the room.

Then a Word of Knowledge came to Elisha that the woman had no child and now her husband was old. "And he said, Call her. And when he had called her, she stood in the door." This time she didn't come into the room because she knew Elisha wanted to repay her and she would have no part in it; his appreciation was enough.

This time Elisha promised her a son. Her eyes widened. "And she said, Nay, my lord, thou man of God, do not lie unto your handmaid" (V.16). What Elisha purposed was beyond her understanding and faith horizon. She and her husband had tried for decades to have a child but with no success. The thought of a child being born in their old age was preposterous.

She felt like Abram and Sari who tried for decades to have a child.

When the Word of Faith came to Abram, all he was anchored to was "seeing I go childless" (Genesis 15:2).

Decades Abram was SEEING his circumstances and not having faith in God! He was caught up in the sense realm of the natural and not the unseen realm of the supernatural.

She knew that Elisha was a man of God; but she also knew that he was human and capable of making mistakes, even lying. She put her foot down: Don't you lie to me! I'm already embarrassed as a woman and it's too painful to talk about! Man of God, don't promise me a blessing, a child that God won't deliver!

According to the Word of the Lord that Elijah spoke she conceived and had a son. Her believing and seeing in the supernatural turned into receiving and seeing in the natural. That day she received revelation of how. Important her thoughts and words were in the Physical realm. She learned to be careful about seeing and believing with the eyes of the soul and body.

Years later, the boy was working with his father in the field and complained that his head was hurting. The father sent him home. There the boy died in her lap. She had waited all these years for a son, and now he lay dead on her lap. It seemed like the Devil had gotten the last laugh: "The nerve of you having a baby when you were denied one by the prince of this world!" The Devil may have whispered in her ear.

But she quickly cast down those thoughts and imaginations. She entered the room that she had sowed into the kingdom and laid the child on the bed of the man of God. She sent a message to her husband to send a laborer and a donkey, so she could ride to Elisha.

When the laborer and donkey arrived, she told the servant to ride hard--not to worry about her, seeing she wasn't a fragile old woman as she may appear to his eye; she was tough and determined to reach the man of God at Mt. Carmel.

> "And she came to the man of God to the hill, she caught him by the feet; but Gehazi came near to thrust her away. And the man of God said, Let her alone; for her soul is vexed within her and the LORD hath hid it from me, and hath not told me. Then she said, Did I desire a son of my lord? Did not I say,

Do not deceive me? (v.27,28).

The Shunammite woman was a foreigner; she had no covenant with God. Nevertheless, God loves the foreigners too. Though the Abrahamic Covenant and the Mosaic Law was given to the children of Israel, it also belonged to the rest of mankind who were wise enough to call upon the Name of the Lord God of Israel.

Though she was a wealthy woman, she had the same reaction to the death of her son as the poor widow of Zidon. She was beyond her human resources to reverse the process of death. The sting of death had vexed her soul, and she felt as though she had been persuaded into believing in hope when there was no hope.

Elisha sent Gehazi with his anointed staff to raise the child from the dead. But Gehazi returned without success. So Elisha went to the child and declared the Name of the Lord. The lad revived and sneezed seven times--the symbol of completion--death was finished in its authority over the child--and the child was raised from the dead. "Then she came in, and fell at his feet, and bowed herself to the ground, and took up her son, and went out" (V.37).

As the Shunammite woman fell at the feet of Elisha and bowed, we need to bow to the Word of God and stop seeing ourselves as weak, sick, poor and in every negative light; we need to start seeing ourselves healed, wealthy and blessed!

This is done by getting off our high horse and falling at the feet of God, and being not faithless but believe His Word, and with a humble heart accept His plans for our lives. There's too much at stake.

The world makes fun of those who think this way: "Seeing the invisible". We're called fanatics, Bible-thumpers; we're called hypocrites because we're not a realistic imitation of Christ to the unsaved. The Word will be taken more seriously by the unsaved world if we live in compliance with it; a good life as a Believer speaks louder than words!

Those who depend on their finances consider Christianity as just another "religion", a crutch for the weak and poor to justify being such; how the rich boast of how they pulled themselves up by their bootstraps--when the truth is many of them inherited it from their pappy!

Ignorantly, they misuse the Name of Jesus as a curse word; they laugh at preachers who strain and wipe the sweat off their foreheads while declaring the gospel of Jesus Christ, and seek to discredit, humiliate the Faith Healers who believe in the Resurrection Anointing, the Holy Spirit of God. These people are spoken against according to the wisdom of this world---until tragedy strikes.

Then desperate words come out of their mouths like, Oh God! Oh Jesus help me! Help, my son is on crack cocaine! Or, my daughter has been in an auto accident! Jesus, it's Cancer, AIDS or any crisis--no matter---it's going to take seeing in the Spirit and believing in the Spirit, in the ways and purposes of God.

The love of God is channeled through us, and manifests in Him not willing that anyone should perish. He's the Savior and forgiver of sins and the Restorer of the breech; He's the Healer, Deliverer, Provider, Resurrection and the Life of the Resurrection Anointing. Sooner or later everyone will need Christ. He's waiting for us to surrender to Him and to meet our every need.

As Abraham sowed his son Isaac and Isaac sowed himself into the Promise, the Father sowed His Seed as an offering and sacrifice for sin. He purposed to reap a harvest of spiritual children. We too must sow good seed into good ground, the kingdom of God, in order to advance its holiness and righteousness on earth as it is in heaven. In this we discover that the Law of Reciprocity--sowing and reaping--is an essential portion of resurrection; it's the planting by faith the natural and reaping the supernatural.

WEEP NOT!

"Weeping may endure for a night, but joy cometh in the morning"
Psalms 30:5 (KJV)

It came to pass in the ministry of Jesus of Nazareth, the Messiah, the Anointed One, as He went about administering the Blessing of the Abrahamic Covenant, He encountered a multitude of diseased and demon-possessed residents of the Physical Realm. This wasn't an unusual occurrence because everyone living on Earth had assorted varieties of demon spirits, and had learned to live in cohabitation with them.

From the days of the Prophet Malachi to the coming of the Prophet John the Baptist heaven was shut and there was no Word from the Ancient One. During this time the Devil had abused mankind, putting upon them heavy yokes and bondages. Christ incarnated specifically to break the Devils back; to minister deliverance to the captives, those who are the heirs of salvation and the prosperous life.

Jesus went about doing His Father's business. Having been Baptized in the Holy Spirit, He was endued with power from on High. He was God-in-the-flesh, being the Word that was made flesh and pitched His tent of flesh, and was made in the likeness of Man for the purpose of fulfilling the righteousness of God. He came to demonstrate the righteousness of God by responding to God's authority with complete obedience; this Adam failed to do.

Adam forfeited the title deed to the Physical Realm and the authority as the god of this realm to Satan. Christ manifested to destroy the works of the Devil; to destroy sickness, disease, poverty, sin and death are the works He will destroy out of the lives of human beings who trusted in His Word.

Multitudes came to Him screaming in misery and pain. He healed them all. His compassion was like warm honey flowing upon their cold lives. He loved them when most didn't love themselves. "For God so loved the world, that He gave His only begotten Son, that whosoever believeth in Him should not perish, but have everlasting life" (John 3:16). He confirmed to the residents that it wasn't the will of the Father that anyone be sick or perish; this was a new doctrine in Israel.

In those days it was difficult for a person with faith to remain sick around Jesus; it was equally difficult to stay dead around Him. The Anointed One sought His level to fill their lives.

Jesus and many of His disciples came into the City of Nain. When He approached the gate of the city, there was a funeral procession coming out. The dead was a woman's only son and she was a widow. She was in a poverty situation, being left with no means of support. Soon the crowd of mourners, relatives and friends would be gone to their own homes and she would be left alone to face an uncertain future.

Perhaps her relatives had large families themselves and couldn't afford to feed another mouth; or perhaps she could imagine herself at the gate called Beautiful, as she had seen others begging for money to buy food.

> "And when the Lord saw her, He had com-passion on her, and said unto her, Weep not. And He came and touched the brier; and they that bare him stood still. And He said, Young man, I say unto thee, Arise. And he that was dead sat up, and began to speak. And He delivered him to his mother" (Luke

7:14,15).

The people declared that God had visited Him people. They knew one of the greatest manifestations of God was the resurrection of the dead.

Another time as Jesus ministered the Word, healed the sick and cast out devils, a man named Jairus, a ruler of the synagogue fell at Jesus' feet, begged Him to come to his house and heal his dying daughter. She was 12 years old; had not yet lived, but was about to die.

Jairus was a humble man. He was respected for his position in the synagogue. He risked his position and even his life by coming to Jesus for help. The Sanhedrin Council forbade the religious leaders from supporting Jesus.

But Jairus was desperate; he no longer cared what the Sanhedrin thought. He would give it all up to have his daughter healed! Tradition was one thing, but the FEAR of the death of his daughter was driving him insane. In front of the crowd, Jairus fell at Jesus' feet and worshipped; definitely a no-no in Israel.

As he pleaded for the life of his daughter, the multitude pressed against Jesus and a woman with internal bleeding touched Him and was healed. Jesus commended her for her great faith. She had made a demand upon His supply of the Anointing and received her healing.

Jairus thought that Jesus didn't hear his petition because the woman engaged Him in conversation. While Jesus spoke to the woman, a messenger came from Jairus' house saying that his daughter was dead; there's no need to trouble Jesus. Nevertheless, Jesus was troubled: Death had challenged Him--mocked Him: Death wanted to operate, business as usual, in the Presence of the Lord of Glory.

Jesus and death had faced off before. As the Christ, He had a four-thousand-year personal vendetta against death; but as Jesus of Nazareth, his personal experience with death came when His stepfather, Joseph died. This happened when Jesus was an adolescent still growing in Grace, knowledge and physical maturity.

Death struck in His own home. The curse of sin and death had been upon the earth since the Garden of Eden and now it had come to His house.

At this time in His life He wasn't empowered to perform miracles: He wasn't Baptized in the Holy Spirit yet. Miracles and His ministry wouldn't commence until He became thirty years old, thus fulfilling the legal and Scriptural requirements of the Mosaic Law.

Concerning the death of Joseph, He could do nothing. (It's also possible that the Heavenly Father would have raised Joseph from the dead if it was in His Divine Plan.) This day He knew what it meant to be Human and experience the loss of a love one.

Though He was the Son of God, He set aside His Deity when He became a man. The part of Him, the Christ, being the Resurrection and the Life had not yet been given back to Him. He felt the pain of separation from Joseph; He experienced the sorrow, vexation and loss; Mary was heart-broken and needed consolation too.

Jesus prayed concerning the Father's will. He received comfort and revelation to help the entire family: Joseph as the guardian of Jesus had to decrease so that God, Jesus' true Father could increase. It was time for Jesus and Mary to depend solely on God and walk by faith alone. Joseph had fulfilled the predestinated paths set for him by God to walk in. Death didn't get the victory in Jesus' family.

As time elapsed, fear came over Jairus. He had waited too long before summoning the Master. His daughter was dead. Death made him feel unclean and defiled.

But Jesus heard his request, though the woman touched Him and virtue released from Him. Jesus also heard the report of the messenger telling Jairus his daughter had died. He said to Jairus, "Fear not: believe only, and she shall be made whole" (Luke 8:50). Jairus rejoiced in his soul and believed the Word that was made flesh and stood before him. Hope sprang up from a hidden well inside of Jairus.

Jesus, Peter, James, John and the parents of the girl went into the house. Everyone around them was weeping and mourning. Jesus said, "Weep not: she is not dead, but sleeps. And they laughed Him to scorn, knowing that she was dead" (V.52, 53).

Jesus put them out! As there's no room for sickness and disease in the kingdom, neither is there room for unbelief. These people were in agreement with death; death was their companion and friend.

Jesus hated death. These scorners were servants of sin and fakes: One minute they were weeping and wailing, the next they were laughing! These doubters wouldn't ruin His resurrection party; their snide remarks grieved the Holy Spirit, actually vexed the Life of Almighty God.

Jesus took the girl's hand and said, "Maid, arise. And her spirit came again, and she arose straightway: and He commanded to give her meat" (V.55,56).

As Christians we will be called upon in the Name of Jesus to pray for the sick or afflicted---even to cast out demons. When we need someone to stand in agreement with us, it wouldn't be wise to choose an unbeliever, a doubter in the miraculous power of God. Hindering spirits and other demonic spirits may work through these individuals to quench the effectiveness of the Holy Spirit. When there are skeptical people in the room, if possible excuse them from the room. Then the Holy Spirit, who would have everyone be saved, delivered, and healed can show His love.

When things go wrong in our lives we must remember that Jesus says, "Fear not, believe only" (Luke 8:50). Drastic situations demand drastic solutions, and Jesus is the solution to life's twists and turns. The scriptures were written to encourage, give us confidence and hope. By this we're certain that Jesus is the same yesterday, today and forever. He cares compassionately, affectionately and watchfully; He won't let us down.

It fell on a day that Lazarus of Bethany was sick. Lazarus, Mary and Martha were close friends of Jesus. They assisted Him in minis-try. Jesus was preaching in the villages beyond the Jordan River near Perea. Jesus received word that one whom He loved was seriously ill and almost dead.

Nevertheless Jesus stayed where He was two more days. Lazarus died. Mary and Martha were heartbroken. When they needed God the most it seemed like He was busy.

In the Spirit, Jesus knew that Lazarus was sick; He also knew that Lazarus would die. But Mary and Martha didn't know the plan of God. His plans weren't based on human relationship, friendship, but upon Covenant, providence, election and predestination.

Lazarus had been dead four days.

When Jesus showed up their faith increased and they could believe anything He said. God was in their Presence (because He was God in the flesh); that Presence soothed the tormented soul and brought peace. Mary and Martha believed that if Jesus had been there Lazarus wouldn't have died. They knew that Jesus was Jehovah-Rapha, the Lord who heals.

Now the revelation came to them that He was the Resurrection and the Life. Of course they knew that Christ would raise His people at the last day, but they hadn't realized He was the Alpha and Omega---Resurrection Day already existed in Him.

Even so, they also believed whatever He asked for the Father would do it; the truth that He and the Father were One Spirit escaped their reasoning, as did many things concerning the Person of the Son of God. Yet their souls rejoiced in His loving kindness and tender mercies. He was Messiah, their inspiration and hope.

Though Mary and Martha testified who He was, they wept for Lazarus as did the other Jews who knew the entire family.

Jesus "groaned in His Spirit and was troubled. Jesus wept. Then said the Jews, Behold how He loved Him!" (v.33,35,36).

He didn't weep because Lazarus was dead; He wept because his death had impacted so many lives. As far as Lazarus was concerned, the groan in His Spirit was the language of "Christ Within" giving the Commandment to raise Lazarus from the dead!

They went to the cave where Lazarus was interned. Jesus told the Jews to take away the stone. Martha protested, saying by now Lazarus stunk. Jesus knew that Lazarus didn't stink any worst than sin stinks in God's nostrils.

He prayed aloud for the benefit of those around Him. His reasons for doing so was to produce Faith in those around Him, and establish a written record of this miracle for generations of people to read and believe. It was also important that the Name, the reputation of God be magnified and established in all the earth.

> "And when He thus had spoken, He cried with a loud voice, Lazarus, come forth. And he that was dead came forth, bound hand and foot with grave clothes; and his face was bound about with a napkin. Jesus said unto them, Loose him, and let him go" (v. 43,44).

Although Lazarus had been raised from the dead, this type of resurrection was only a temporary one. Lazarus would one day die a permanent physical death.

God. Later, with the deterioration of his "dirt" body, he succumb-bed to old age and then physical death.

With Salvation, comes the reversal of the process of the Law of Sin and Death; it's the resurrection of the spirit body.

If the spirit body isn't resurrected before the physical body dies, the soul--without the "quickened" spirit body--- will stand before the White Throne Judgment Seat of the Lord Jesus Christ, and will be judged for not being in compliance with the Word of God concerning the Resurrection of the spirit body; then condemned to eternity in Hell, which is the final death.

Many point out scriptures and believe that Hell is a place where the soul is tormented throughout eternity; others point out different scriptures and believe that at some point in eternity Hell and those in it are completely destroyed--thus no "everlasting" torment, but complete obviation.

Still there are others who believe that Hell is like our prison system with different levels of incarceration and punishments; the worst of Hell is for the most wicked sinners, down to the least who merely refused to accept Jesus Christ as their personal Lord and Savior and walk in His commandments.

But what in Hell do we want? There is nothing in Hell we want! Why go there to discover which theory is correct? It's like experimenting with deadly poisons to discover which one torments and then kills you the fastest!

Before the New Testament Covenant with Salvation arrived, Sheol was the resting place for the dead. From Adam to Jesus of Nazareth, Sheol was the far country for those who had sinned and fallen short of the glory of God. Other than Jesus, there was no one who didn't sin and miss the mark.

On the mount where Jesus was transfigured, appeared Moses and Elijah who talked to Jesus. These residents of Sheol with the other pro-phets, priests and kings of Israel were likely the government of the Israeli territory of the Sheol kingdom--but Satan was their overlord. Sheol, though often called paradise, wasn't heaven and definitely fell short of being Hell. Sheol was a temporary "weigh station" between Heaven and Hell until the gospel of the kingdom of God could be preached. Then the great and fortunate opportunity to receive Salvation, the Resurrection of the Human Spirit and an inheritance in Heaven would be available. The inhabitants of Sheol were captives, prisoners of war, the war between Good and Evil.

Adamic Death held them there; like chains holding a convicted criminal, the Enforcer of the Law wouldn't release them; Death wanted its pound of flesh, and personal sins added to the weight of the chains as death reigned through sin.

Notes

CHAPTER THREE
THE WORD WAS MADE FLESH

4 "Surely He hath borne our grief's, and carried our sorrows; yet we did esteem Him stricken, smitten of God, and afflicted. 5 But He was wounded for our transgressions, He was bruised for our iniquities; the chastisement of our peace was upon Him; and with His stripes we are healed" Isa. 53.4 (KJV).

Six hundred years before Calvary, the Prophet Isaiah saw in a vision the suffering Savior of the world being crucified for the sins of mankind. We can only imagine the horror and awe in Isaiah's mind as the Spirit of God unfolded the events; the Father opened up Isaiah's spiritual eyes and revealed a portion of the Mystery.

Isaiah saw the Servant of God as an object of horror. His face and body was marred, disfigured and distorted beyond what could naturally befall a man. He was cursed with calamity more than any Human could endure and survive. His whole body was busted and bleeding profusely. His wounds weren't entirely from those who abused and crucified Him, but even generational curses from the Garden of Eden fell upon his tormented soul and body. Adamic Sin was placed upon Him, and this brought spiritual death to His Human spirit; the Spirit of the Lord departed from Him; and this death was the first offering.

Then all the sins, iniquity, and trespasses committed from Adam to the last person leaving the Physical Realm, the personal sins of the human souls of mankind impregnated with the nature of the Tree of the Knowledge of Good and Evil, was heaved upon Him and nailed to the cross:

This included rebellion, pride, fears self-centeredness, lusts, un-forgiveness, perversions, and addictions of the flesh, anger, greed, mental and emotional illnesses; and every curse that can be named and known to weaken or destroy Man was nailed to the Cross.

When He physically died, the traumas of the physical life, diseases of the past, present, and future were thrust upon Him. This included cancers, blindness, deafness, blood and bone diseases, organ damage and deformities; and every sickness, virus and infirmity that can be named was healed in Jesus Christ.

Jesus of Nazareth sowed His entire Person as an offering for our sins and it was accepted by the Father; for it pleased the Lord to inflict Him and make Him an offering for our sins. These three offerings appeased the indictment of God and settled the long-overdue sin account. By faith in the finished work of the cross, we were healed and made whole.

The truth is that the Savior of the world, Jesus Christ is still despised and rejected. People still don't believe or appreciate Him and what He accomplished on the cross at Calvary. He bore our sins, sicknesses and diseases; He bore the punishment for our disobedience; He fulfilled the righteousness of the Mosaic Law which we couldn't keep because we're weak in the flesh; and His Blood was the ONLY ATONEMENT that God would accept. He took our weaknesses and gave us His strong righteousness.

Now, through faith in Him we're His spiritual offspring, being the children of the resurrection, and the fruit of the Seed.

Isaiah sounded the depths of God's Spirit, and the Spirit of God brought forth further revelation: "The people that walk in darkness have seen a great Light: they that dwell in the land of the shadow of death, upon them hath the Light shined. For unto us a child is born, unto us a son is given; and the government shall be upon His shoulder: and His Name shall be called Wonderful, Counselor, The Mighty God, The Everlasting Father, The Prince of Peace (Isaiah 9:2,6). And it shall come to pass in that day, that his (Satan's) burden shall he taken away from off thy (our) shoulders, and his yoke from off thy neck, and THE YOKE SHALL BE DESTROYED BECAUSE OF THE ANOINTING" (Isaiah 10:27).

This was similar to the prophesy and song that Zacharias the priest and father of John the Baptist gave. The people who sat in darkness saw a great Light. This great Light gave knowledge of Salvation and forgiveness of sins. John would prepare the way for the Lord Jesus Christ, Whose Name is Wonderful, Counselor, The Mighty God, The Everlasting Father, and the Prince of Peace. His spiritual government is the Church; the Church extends into the Physical Realm, where the satanic yokes thrust upon us are destroyed because of our Faith in Jesus Christ, the Messiah.

Isaiah wasn't the only one who tapped into the hidden treasures of God. God revealed another portion of His Mystery; He gave prophesies to several of the Old Testament saints who were instrumental to His plans. Daniel was a prophet whom the Lord blessed with visions and revelations.

Daniel was a faithful prophet of God. He saw the Divine Man sitting on the Throne: All the nations of the world worshipped Him. His kingdom was an everlasting dominion which shall never pass away. He also saw the Saints (us) of the Most High forever possessing the kingdom (Dan. 7:14-18).

The divine drama continues. Only those determined to know Jesus Christ and the power of His Resurrection dared to search and inquire of God about the Mystery that was hidden for ages but was revealed to the prophets of God.

The Lamb of God slain from the foundation of the world was methodically becoming reality in the natural world. Daniel saw the Son of God receive from the Father glory, honor, dominion and an everlasting kingdom. He also saw Satan Humiliated, defeated, and all nations and peoples bowed before Christ, the Son of God.

Daniel saw the Saints of God, the Church receive our inheritance from the Son who brought us into unity with the Father; the Son baptized the Saints in the Holy Spirit and made us like Himself and the Father; we the Saints became joint-heirs to rule the dominion with Him, and share in His righteous authority.

The Apostle John experience Christ in a different way. He declared: "In the beginning was the Word and the Word was with God, and the Word was God...All things were made by Him"(Jn. 1.1,3). Which left no room for anyone else to shoulder creation, or any evolution theory of scientific speculations.

The Apostle John diligently prepared his case. His opening statement was to build a foundation of reference. He wrote that the eternal Word was the foundation of Creation; and the Word was Christ, also called the Messiah, the Anointed One.

John went on to confirm that Christ was God Himself, and this Word/Christ became a Human being, whose identity was later revealed as Jesus of Nazareth. He was the Human vessel in which the Word used to cloth Himself in humanity---the flesh. Now He, the

Word was legally a resident here, being born of a woman. This was the perfect way for God to fellowship and talk to His people: As one of them who ate, slept and breathed the same air.

"Forever, 0 Lord, thy Word is settled in heaven" (Ps. 119:89). God's Word is complete and is settled in His mind. He's the Ancient One who inhabits eternity; yet He condescended to be as a man to lead and guild us away from darkness into His marvelous Light. Therefore, David said, "Thy Word is a lamp unto my feet and a light upon our path" (Ps. 119:105).

Christ, the Word of God is highly exalted. God's Name depends on the immutability, unchanging nature of His Word. For all things begin and end in Christ the Word.

God who is rich in mercy, expressed His love, power, riches, grace and kindness towards us in giving Jesus Christ.

Through the process of spiritual adoption all Believers are temples of God. The same way the Spirit of God dwelled in Jesus of Nazareth, our example, the Spirit dwells in us.

As the block and masonry temple of God was a sacred place, the Human temple must be thought of and regarded as sacred---even the unborn babies.

Contrary to popular belief, the truth remains that God is only the Father of His children, the Christians; Satan is the father of those who aren't Born Again (Jn. 8:44). God will not claim anyone as His legitimate seed, unless they have the Holy Spirit. Otherwise, they are only potential sons and daughters.

We call God "Father" because He's our Spiritual Father; but if we were spiritually dead and unsaved, then technically He's not our Father until we have His Spirit living in us.

We all had natural Human fathers (though we may not know who he is)who helped bring us into the natural world; and according to the flesh, all men are truly brothers. But according to the Word of God, Christians are New Creatures, New Creations---even a new species of life in the world. Therefore, only those who are in Christ are of and in the same Spiritual Family.

The Apostle John stated that the Children of God aren't born by sexual union: "Which were born, not of blood, nor of the will of the flesh, nor of the will of man, but of God" (Jn. 1:13).

Therefore, joining a church doesn't make us Christians, Children of God, but by receiving His Holy Spirit; without the indwelling Holy Spirit, we're just playing pretend church as pretend Christians.---mere actors and actresses playing a part.

THE MINISTRY OF JESUS CHRIST

John Baptized the people in the Jordan River. The Father appointed him to prepare the way for the Lord Jesus Christ. John baptized the believers who repented of their sins and were godly sorry for them, sorry enough to quit living the lawless lifestyle.

As John baptized for the remission of sins, his message was repentance prepared the way for the spirit, soul, and body to receive the Lord; it was not an outward sign, but also an inward experience. John's message was a simple one: REPENT, for the kingdom of heaven is at hand.

Repentance wasn't a complicated message yet dynamic in its results; for the Lord had suddenly come into His Holy Temple. John told his new converts, "I indeed baptize you with water unto repentance: but He that cometh after me is mightier than I, whose shoes I am not worthy to bear: He shall baptize you with the Holy Ghost, and with fire" (Mat. 3:11).

John the Baptist water baptized Jesus of Nazareth in the Jordan River. This was Jesus' ordination ceremony: "And the Holy Ghost descended in a bodily shape like a dove upon Him, and a voice came from heaven, which said, Thou art My Son; in whom I am well pleased" (Lk. 3:22).

Children of God are recreated individuals, created by God and not by manmade services, ceremonies, or mere attendance in a church or other religious gatherings. Though the major religions of the earth claim that God (or another form of the Name) is their spiritual Father, it's an empty claim.

By the cover of darkness Nicodemus came to Jesus and asked, "How can a man be born when he is old? Can he enter his mother's womb and be born?" Jesus replied, "Unless a man is born of water and [even] the Spirit, he cannot [ever] enter the Kingdom of God." Old "Nick at Night" questioned, "How can all this be possible?" (Jn. 3:4,5,9).

Nicodemus was totally confused. The rebirth of Man just didn't make sense. Until Jesus began teaching all over Israel, Nicodemus and the other Doctors of the Law thought that their decades of study, teachings and lecturing on the Mosaic Law and the Prophets was more important than anything else; his Doctorate Degree qualified him as an expert in theology and religious interpretations.

But lately many of Jesus' teachings had reached the ears of the Sanhedrin Council--and caused plenty of controversy. Nicodemus purposed in his heart to personally speak with this young Teacher from Galilee.

A multitude of thoughts went through his hoary head; some of the thoughts favored believing on Jesus; some of the thoughts doubted that He was who He said He was.

However, this Jesus of Nazareth performed several notable miracles. Even the Sanhedrin wouldn't deny that He performed the acts, though they condemned the healings because many were done on the Sabbath Day, a day of rest and reflection, a day when one should stay sick and hope not to die before Morning!

The Sanhedrin also refuted His claims that He came down from heaven, that He was the Son of God, Son of Man, that God was His Father, therefore making Himself equal with God, plus other claims of divinity.

Could Jesus really be the Messiah, the Son of God? Or perhaps this Jesus, like the previous impostors who claimed to be some great personality, but only deceived the people by performing magic tricks; or placed healthy accomplices in the crowds, then claimed healing.

Nicodemus remembered the star in the sky thirty-three years ago, when the Sanhedrin debated about the Messiah being born in Bethlehem, Judea... Jesus was the right age.

With all these thoughts going through Nicodemus' head, in the cover of darkness he spoke with the Master. Nicodemus came at night to avoid harassment or being forced to resign from the Council. But after listening to Jesus, he failed to comprehend through reasoning the paradox of the rebirth, that the rebirth wasn't a physical but spiritual experience. The rebirth, Jesus told him was absolutely necessary before ever seeing or being acquainted with God and His Kingdom. Nicodemus didn't have a clue what Jesus was talking about, but he felt in his soul a need to know. Nicodemus was young but remembered the Star of Bethlehem, and how the Sanhedrin was fearful of the coming Messiah. He wondered was Jesus of Nazareth the One who escaped King Herod's Decree.

Since the Kingdom of God is within, certain inner preparations have to be made: That decision constitutes the Negative Confession, a confession of sins; then the Positive Confession, a confession of Faith in Jesus Christ. The Holy Spirit who searches our heart knows whether we're sincere about both confessions, whether the confessions are of the heart or of the head.

Satisfied with the search, the Holy Spirit recreates our Human spirit and makes His abode there. The instant the Holy Spirit arrives the door to the Kingdom opens; that Door is Christ (Jn. 10:7). Through the open Door, the Kingdom of God can be truly experienced while we're still living on earth.

The rivers of living waters flows from beneath the Throne in Heaven, through the open Door and into the regenerated human spirit; then the river flows into the soul, physical body then out into the world. As temples of God we often see visions of our heavenly home, angels, relatives, and of course--Jesus!

Jesus explained to Nicodemus that such a Born Again person is like the wind. The wind is mysterious and no one knows where it comes from or the secrets of where it has been; the wind cannot be seen but observed as it moves things or is felt as it comes in contact with the human body; if the wind were intelligent, imagine what knowledge and wisdom it would have of its adventures and scenic routes to the top of mountains and lower valleys; and so is everyone a Mystery who is born of the Spirit of God.

Jesus told Nicodemus that unless he was Born Again he couldn't "enter" into the Kingdom of God. The Kingdom of God exists as an experience--a state of being, as reality of a different spiritual order of life, in our re-created spirit; the Kingdom is righteousness, peace, and joy in the Holy Ghost.

The Kingdom of God is also an inhabited realm, a place and reality of existence dimensions above the physical realm; it's a place of eternal rest and bliss; there's no evil, no crime, no sickness, no pain, no Devil! Heaven has building structures, mountains, meadows, rivers, gardens and a sky that never darkens. Heaven's capitol city is New Jerusalem. But above all, the Kingdom of Heaven is where the Throne is, where Jehovah-Elohim sits in unity with the Divine Man, the Savior Christ the Word. Jesus counseled Nicodemus. He told the aged Doctor that his many years of religious doctrines were unprofitable; he told Nicodemus, like a newborn babe, he had to start all over.

All the self-life accomplishments must experience death; that as an individual person he must be nailed fastidiously on the cross, as a spiritual criminal having no merit or redeemable qualities; that Jehovah-Elohim, being no respecter of persons, wouldn't look his way favorably because he was a member of the Sanhedrin or a ruler of the Jews:

> "Let not the wise man glory in his wisdom, neither let the mighty man glory in his might, let not the rich man glory in his riches; but let him that glory, glory in this, that he hath understanding, and knows Me" (Jer. 9:23).

Jesus understood that Nicodemus taught what he knew from the Law and the Prophets; but John the Baptist, the last of the Old Testament Prophets---preached what the prophets before him only prophesied: Repentance, the Kingdom of Heaven and the Lamb of God is at hand!

Nicodemus, as you listened and quoted from your favorite prophets---listen to John too; for John was the bridge between the Old Testament and New Testament prophets and prophecies.

You taught in the synagogues week after week and year after year--but you didn't *hear* the voice of the prophets whom you quoted with ease.

But it's not too late Nicodemus, not late to intimately know the Lord as your Savior and Passport into the Kingdom; but always remember that everything else is vanity.

Nicodemus left Jesus with a humbled spirit. The questions and desires of his heart were satisfied. Now he knew that Jesus was the Messiah, because He spoke directly to his heart, and his heart believed and received His witness.

Nicodemus also understood who the Children of God really are, that they are not birthed according to the flesh, but nevertheless are the true seed of Abraham according to Faith in the Messiah. He went away a lot wiser than when he arrived.

Now Jesus of Nazareth, the Seed, a Man Anointed with the Holy Spirit began to minister under the provisions of the Abrahamic Covenant, the first Covenant activated and energized by Faith.

This was the Blessing spoke of in Deuteronomy Chapter 28:1-14. That if the children of Israel would obey the Commandments, the Lord Jesus Christ would set us above the nations.

All the blessings in the storehouses of God would come upon us and overtake us. We would be blessed in the cities and in the country; our children, crops, livestock, finances and investments would be multiplied; we would be blessed going in and out of our homes. The Abrahamic Covenant (within the New Testament Covenant) declared that our enemies who rise up against us would advance one way but flee from us seven ways!

Because He could verify this by no greater than Himself; the God who cannot lie promised to establish His children in holiness and righteousness, because we call on His Name.

Jesus proclaimed in the synagogue: "The Spirit of the Lord is upon Me, because He hath anointed Me to preach the gospel to the poor; He hath sent Me to heal the brokenhearted, to preach deliverance to the captives, and recovering of sight to the blind, to set at liberty them that are bruised, To preach the acceptable year of the Lord" (Luke 4:18,19). He closed the Book of Isaiah and sat down: This scripture was eternally fulfilled.

The people were astonished at the gracious words that flowed from His mouth, "for His Word was with power" (v.32). The people were further amazed, saying, "What a Word is this! For with Authority and Power He commands the unclean spirits, and they come out" (v.36). Devils came out crying "You are Christ the Son of God. And He rebuked them suffered them not to speak; for they knew that He was Christ" (v.41).

Though the unclean spirits knew who He was, the Children of Israel didn't. His determined purpose in ministry was to change that. He came to turn the whole world upside down. Upon Christ the solid Rock of Ages, He would build His Church, and the gates of Hell would not prevail against it.

The demons had "knowledge" of Him but no Faith in Him; the Children of Israel also had knowledge of the scriptures but failed to recognize Him and lacked genuine Faith.

Therefore, He prepared for them a solid foundation built upon Faith in Him: For "without faith it is impossible to please God" (Hebrews 11:6). Jesus truly wanted the children of Israel to please God. Soon they learned to trust and rely upon Him. During His ministry, He preached the kingdom was at hand. Whosoever desired to see and enter into the kingdom must be Born Again.

He taught them the First Commandment was to love God, their neighbor as themselves. Jesus went about binding up the broken hearted, proclaiming liberty to the captives, those who were bound by Satan through sicknesses, diseases, poverty, and the grave. He said that whom the Son has set free was free indeed.

Jesus not only talked a good talk but walked a holy walk. He was anointed; He literally opened up the mental and emotional prisons of the mind and freed the Jews from Satan and his devils.

Jesus comforted the lonely, the oppressed and those who had lost all hope in life. He brought beauty for ashes--restored what the locus had eaten up! He reconciled marriages and families, resurrected dreams that were long dead. And in so doing, He clothed the citizens in joy, a garment of praise for the spirit of heaviness. His Life was a living testimony to God's love for Man.

"When the Evening was come, they brought unto Him many that were possessed with devils; and He cast out the spirits with His Word, and healed all that were sick: That it might be fulfilled which was spoken by Isaiah the prophet, saying, Himself took our infirmities, and bare our sicknesses" (Matthew 8:16,17).

Jesus explained to Israel the reason why they suffered calamity wasn't because God didn't love them but they continuously rebelled against His authority, and the curses described in Deuteronomy listed after the "blessings" had come upon them and overtaken them.

He advised them that if they would believe on His Name, all things were possible to them that believed; if they would cleave to, trust in and rely on Him, they would be saved and not come into condemnation; for in Him is no rejection; but if they wouldn't believe, they were already judged, convicted and waiting for the sentence to be carried out.

The legal basis for God's indictment for sin, why and how Israel was judged lies in this: Christ, the Light has come into the world, and Israel has habitually loved the darkness rather and more than the light, because the Jews didn't want to stop serving their own self-interest and the Devil. Their religious leaders loved the attention and power of their various titles. They told others how to live and what to do.

Many people didn't want to hear Jesus' sermons. The religious Pharisees and Sadducees stalked and conspired to murder Him. Never theless, Jesus didn't soften or sugarcoat His messages of hope, redemption, and eternal judgment.

"And Jesus said unto them, I am the Bread of Life; he that cometh to Me shall never hunger; and he that believeth on Me shall never thirst" (John 6:35). He was the Life-Giving and sustaining manna the Father gave Israel to eat as they journeyed through the Wilderness of Sin. Jesus also told them in no uncertain terms: "...except ye eat the flesh of the Son of man and drink His blood, ye have no life in you" (John 6:53).

As the Light of the World, He told them that He was that inexhaustible Light and the Life of men. "And the Light shines in the darkness, and the darkness comprehended it not" (John 1:4,5). He taught that a Believer in Him was a city on a hill and couldn't be hid; and a Believer was the Salt of the earth.

As the Way, Truth and Life, He told them, "No man comes unto the Father, but by Me" (John 14:6). This surprised the people for there were many religions and paths claiming to lead to God. But Jesus proved that God was with Him and the others were liars.

As the Good Shepherd, He disclosed His mission: "I am the Good Shepherd; the Good Shepherd gives His life for the sheep" (John 10:11). The Shepherd loves the sheep but a hireling is in it for profit, and would betray the sheep to the Wolf--Satan.

As to His Deity, He didn't keep it secret: "I and the Father are One. I am the Son of God" (John 10:30,36). He didn't claim God was only His natural Father, but God was also His co-equal, because He was the Word that was in the beginning with God.

The religious leaders had a fit over His equality statement concerning God. To them it was the worst of blasphemes: A man claiming he's God? They burned hot with indignation, rage made their eyes large, bloodshot and demonic in character; murder was in those eyes. Their determined purpose was to kill Him! To them, killing Jesus was doing God a favor, when in fact, it was only keeping the present religious order in power.

As to the Resurrection of Life, He advised them to check His credentials with the widow of Nain, Jairus, Lazarus and his relatives. Then return and follow Him in the Resurrection of Life.

As the True Vine, he proclaimed: "I am the Vine, you are the branches: He that abides in Me, and I in him, the same brings forth much fruit; for without Me, you can do nothing" (John 15:5). He made it perfectly clear.

As he ministered throughout the region, it was apparent He wasn't fond of religion; religion was a waste of the measure of Faith the Father gave to all people.

Jesus didn't come here to start another religion, but to put mankind's hand into God's hands, so they could walk together in Covenant; for how can two walk together unless they agree?

Jesus' ministry was one of reconciliation. Therefore, He wasn't a religious man but a man who valued prayer and personal relationships. He had a personal relationship with the Father and encouraged everyone to seek the same.

The path to the heart of the Father was through faith, obedience and love. Jesus said, "If any man will come after Me, let him deny himself, and take up his cross and follow Me" (Lk. 9:23).

This passage was written to all Believers who are determined to know Christ. We must learn to deny our self-life and interests, be broken by crucifixion, reckoning ourselves as dead to sin and temptations; this is done by faith. We must also be available and willing in spirit, soul, and body to be changed into the image of Jesus.

The determined purpose that the Apostle Paul had must also be our tireless goal. Knowing the Person of Christ brings enormous understanding and freedom from fear; the breaking of the outer man releases the Spirit; He rushes forth changing us, situations, circumstances and the world around us.

The cross and the crucified, unselfish life is the key to survival in this dark world. In the time of weakness and humility, brings the desire to lay down our lives for the Gospel of Christ, the outer man is broken and the Spirit is released; in the same manner the young chick cannot be free until the eggshell around it is broken.

Jesus said that we're the Light of the World. If we abide in Him, we shall not walk in darkness but shall have the Light of Life. Living the humble, obedient, crucified life brings forth the Resurrection Anointing; and Resurrection is Life, as Christ is the Life of the Resurrection; Christ is the Anointing. Paul wrote, "I am crucified with Christ" (Gal. 2:20). He said that the

the Life he now lived he lived by Faith in Jesus Christ. He didn't continue to live the old life but the new one.

Jesus tells us to live the crucified and consecrated life. The entrance into the Life of Christ hasn't changed; it will not change, for God cannot change. So as long as we're chasing our own dreams---being preoccupied with family, social engagements, friends, career, and become unavailable for our Calling; and continuously walking after the flesh---nothing is going to change in our lives.

Denying the pleasure senses and its passions releases the Life of Christ in us to do the perfect will of God.

The Mystery will always be Christ and not ourselves; for of ourselves we can do nothing of heavenly value. When God is glorified then our light will shine.

We're the temple of the living God, a temple God will occupy if we let Him. It's the Lord Jesus Christ who blessed us with heaped-up spiritual blessings in Him.

It wasn't our family, friends, job or our own ingenuity that brought this utterly wonderful blessing of regeneration and Hope in our lives.

> "Verily, verily, I say unto you, except a corn of wheat fall to the earth and die, it abides alone; but if it die, it brings forth much fruit" Jn. 12.24 (KJV).

In the allegory of the grain of wheat Jesus gave us the key to unlock the storehouse that contains the hidden Mystery. He foretold the process by which He would conquer death.

The life of the grain of wheat is sealed and contained in its outer earthen shell. The potential for life is hidden, stored up and waiting to be released. All that the seed will ever become, the potential for even the tallest tree is contained in the seed.

Non-Christian and Christian are seeds. The difference between the two is the Non-Christian haven't been planted in the rich soil of the Word of God, and so doesn't release their maximum potential, so they experience limited growth. The Christian as seed is planted and the potential is released into abundant growth.

The natural seed is planted in fertile ground where the external forces of nature, the moist, dark environment causes the outer shell to split open and die; then the hidden life within the seed uses the dead mass, the planted body to release the new life. The new, resurrected life pushes upward until it breaks through the surface of the ground and establishes itself.

Jesus symbolically explained to the people His death on the cross. Crucifixion was punishment for criminals, there was also a curse put upon the recipients; Jesus explained beforehand that His death would be different and accomplish a divine purpose: The Resurrection Anointing of God would be released, causing many identical seeds, many sons to share in the Resurrection by the Spirit of God. But if Jesus, as the lone Seed wasn't planted in the ground through death, He would live but as only one Seed.

"Which none of the princes of this world knew; for had they known it, they would not have crucified the Lord of glory" (I Corinthians 2:8). Had the demonic princes known that Jesus was the Seed who would die and manifest in the Physical Realm the Mystery and the Resurrection Anointing, they wouldn't have crucified Him; the princes would have preferred Him to live in the flesh forever.

The humbling of the outer person, the death of self, releases the Anointing. Having a determined purpose to know the Christ that resides in every Born Again Believer creates the ideal environment to bring forth the expected results.

It's not that other Christians have a natural ability in spiritual matters, but some of us are more willing, dedicated to sacrifice our self-interest and spend quality time pursuing the Lord until He possesses us and we Him. Losing interest and the love of the world, and gaining interest and the love for Christ is a giant step in the right direction.

The ministry of Jesus Christ continues on the earth. His evangelical ministry by the Holy Spirit is healing, restoration, teaching and preaching; He has the tremendous task to change us into the image of Christ.

ALL MEN SEEK FOR THEE

"And when they found Him, they said unto Him, All men seek for thee" Luke. 1:37 (KJV)

The disciples of Jesus Christ: Matthew, Mark, Luke, and John took pen and wrote about the birth, preparation, message, ministry, then His death and resurrection. Christ is the Ancient One Who became flesh and walked the Earth for thirty-three wonderful years. Because of the greatness of His Person, each writer received a different revelation from the Father about His Son. The brain of a Human Being cannot comprehend or contain all that the Person, the Deity of Jesus Christ, the Messiah is eternally.

Matthew saw Him as the King with a genealogy from Abraham and the throne of King David. Though Jesus was born right under their noses, the Jews didn't recognize their Messiah because He didn't fit "their image" of a Conquering King. Matthew saw Him as the Conquering King, who reigns in the hearts of His children; Who is the Blessed Hope, King of Kings and Lord of Lords.

As the Christian Army we have our orders to occupy until Jesus returns. We enforce the victory won by Jesus Christ at Calvary. We await the day when our mortality will put on immortality and newness of Eternal Life.

"For even the Son of man came not to be ministered unto, but to minister, and to give His life a ransom for many" (Mark 10:45). Mark saw Jesus as the Servant. He concentrated on Jesus' servant heart. Christ humbled Himself and became a man in order to serve man.

He taught by example that the greatest spiritual position a person can acquire is to be a servant of mankind. Jesus taught humility as the way to be exalted by the Father. He also used numerous parables to describe the Kingdom of God and its righteousness.

Jesus was bold and courageous; He taught as One having authority. His knowledge wasn't secondhand; He knew God personally, because He was God Himself. At the end of Mark's account of the gospel, he wrote about Jesus dying on the cross for the sinners He loved and served.

> "And Jesus said unto him, This day is salvation come to this house forasmuch as he also is a son of Abraham. For the Son of man is come to seek and to save that which was lost" (Luke19:9,10).

Luke saw Jesus Christ as the Savior of the world. Luke affirmed Christ's Deity, that He was also the Son of God and, because of His humanity, the Son of man. Luke was a Greek (the only known Gentile writer in the New Testament) physician, a man of natural science and trained as an objective observer.

He wasn't superstitious or a religious man; no one could cleverly devise false sicknesses, diseases, healings or deaths; no illusionist or magician could fool him. Luke wrote of Jesus' authenticity, His relationships with people, prayer and miracles. Jesus gave a prominent place to woman. Luke received revelation of Christ as Jehovah-Rapha, the Lord Who Heals, and this moved him to write in detail the miraculous Jesus Christ.

We as Christians must also receive the revelation that the Lord Jesus can and will heal His people, for He is no respecter of persons. He's the same yesterday, today, and forever. What He has done for others He will do for us.

> "And many other signs, truly did Jesus in the presence of His disciples, which are not written in this book. But these are written, that you might believe that Jesus is the Christ, the Son of God; and that believing you might have life through His Name" (John 20:30,31).

John, the disciple "whom Jesus loved" saw Jesus as the Word of God that was made flesh. John received the revelation that all things were created by the Word.

He also saw Jesus as the Light of the World; this Light couldn't be comprehended, absorbed, appropriated or put out by Satan and the powers of darkness. John showed a contrast between the Light representing those who received Christ, and darkness representing those who love Satan more and rather than Christ, because, unfortunately, they don't want to change.

The Blessing, the Promise of God was embodied in His Son. Salvation came to the human race in the Person of Jesus Christ, the eternal Truth.

John also saw Jesus Christ as the Lamb of God, Bread, Vine, Gate, and the Resurrection and the Life. John wrote that Jesus had divine Agape Love for all people. His tears, compassion and warmth wooed John to love Him with all his heart. John laid his head upon Jesus' chest at the Last Supper.

We must love the Lord like John loved Him with a quiet trust in His every Word. We must also be sincere in our Praise and Worship, remembering if it were not for Him, we'd be dead in our sins and trespasses.

And waiting for Hell to be our permanent home.

All men seek after Him: John realized the prophetic nature of his words. True, he and his company *were* searching for Jesus--but it's also written and predestined that Man seek the Lord wherever He may be found.

As the multitudes in ancient times sought to know Him, and His disciples received revelations pertaining to His Person--every soul journeying through the Physical Realm is looking for Jesus Christ; but not everyone knows it's Jesus Christ they seek.

The unsaved multitudes seek answers to the ancient question: What is life? This question fuels numerous other questions until even nature volunteers to answer some of them.

The masses wander the face of the earth searching for love, peace of mind, security, health, wealth, and a guarantee there's more to life than what's seen with the eyes. Some believe in God, Heaven, Hell, angels, and demons--but disagree on the most important question: Is Jesus Christ the Lord God?

The sublime need of the Human spirit and soul is confirmation that Jesus Christ is God: Man needs to be filled with Christ. Everyone agrees that mortal life in this world ends with the death of the physical body; what would be the great wisdom of God to create life within us, as short as it is in this realm, and provide no continuation of life in a higher realm of consciousness? Yet, many who believe in a heavenly afterlife, don't want to prepare for the journey!

Everyone is looking for Jesus; many search for His kingdom in the wrong places. Some look for Him only in the realm of the flesh, the pseudo pleasures of drugs, alcohol, sexual immorality, money, politics, career, crime, and religions. But all these things are traps. Christ isn't found in these things.

He's not found at the bottom of a whiskey bottle, or in the ashes of a crack pipe; or the going from lover to lover. In the long run nothing can take the place of Christ in us; absolutely nothing. Sin leads to death and Hell, not Christ and Heaven.

THE LAMB FOR SINNERS SLAIN

22 "Pilate said unto them, What shall I do with Jesus? 24...Let Him be crucified. 25 ...His blood be on us, and on our children"

children" Matthew 27:22,24,25 (KJV)

Pontius Pilate, the Governor of Judea was in an awkward position. He knew that Jesus was innocent---even Pilate's Jewish wife, who knew her people well---told him not to listen to the Sanhedrin Council who used their influence to get rid of opposition; don't be used and do their dirty work for them! It's a religious conspiracy against an innocent man!. Both knew that envy and jealousy was at the root of the accusation against Jesus of Nazareth.

But Pilate's appointment as governor depended on him keeping the peace in the region. At any cost, his duty was to suppress riots, crimes, and preserve the Roman Military Occupation. So, in the presence of the angry mob, he washed his hands of the whole matter.

Pilate wasn't surprised as the behavior of the Jews; he knew their history and traditions. Pilate knew that the Jews claimed to be the chosen people of God; and they would rather free Barabbas, a murderous scoundrel, instead of Jesus of Nazareth, a man of peace and good works.

Pilate, a Roman, knew the Roman gods were sometimes cruel and heartless, but they were outmatched by these treacherous Jews. Pilate let the Sanhedrin decision stand: "His blood be on us, and on our children," is what the Jews shouted; Pilate felt sorry for their children (many theologians believe that the curse of these words spoken against Jesus manifested in Germany when 6 million Jews were killed by Hitler's Nazi Party.

After Jesus had been brutally beaten, He was crucified upon a cross outside of Jerusalem at a place called Gogotha, which means the place of the skull. Suspended between heaven and earth, He bled and suffered the curse of the forsaken.

He uttered many gracious words like, "Father, forgive them, for they know not what they do" (Luke 23:34). That statement annoyed many of the bystanders. The religious leaders mocked Jesus; they expected Him to confess he was a fraud and plead to save His life, but He didn't; so then they assumed He would play the blasphemous Son of God role to the death; never once considering that He was the Son of God spoken of by all the prophets. The religious had no pity or compassion for Him.

His Roman executioners couldn't tolerate Jesus making such humble comments. Throughout the years they performed hundreds of crucifixions; criminals cursed and swore obscenities, even threatened to return from the grave to murder them--but that was only talk--not one of them ever returned from the grave.

Yet, Jesus didn't curse them. He said profound things like: "My God, My God, why hast Thou forsaken Me?" (Matthew 27:46). Some thought He called for Elijah, but He was talking to His Father; others thought that Jesus was asking God to miraculously remove Him from the cross. The Romans waited; no one came to His rescue.

Then He said, "It is finished" (John 19:30). What's finished? How can He finish anything while hanging on a cross? Did He mean that He was finished--death had finally gotten Him? Or had He lost so much blood He became delirious?

In the invisible, Satan and his cohorts laughed. They were the ones who incited the Jews against Jesus; they were the ones who secretly stalked Jesus since the day He was born in Bethlehem.

Satan personally entered Judas Iscariot (Luke 22:3) and, for thirty pieces of silver, Judas betrayed the innocent blood to Caiaphas, the High Priest. After Satan was done with Judas Iscariot, persuaded him to hang himself.

Jesus cried, "Father, into Thy hands I commend My Spirit" (Luke 23:46). Then He gave up the ghost. The Roman executioners knew that Jesus was innocent of breaking any Roman Laws; they beat Him because it was their duty and they enjoyed it; they crucified Him because it was ordered by Pontius Pilate; and dealing with the San-hedrin, the religious leaders, executing innocent people was often unavoidable.

Mock trials were commonplace as the rich and influential perverted justice. But they had never heard a condemned man speak so kindly in the midst of suffering and death. What further made this execution one for the record books was the fact the sun refused to shine. There wasn't a cloud in the sky, and it was dark from three in the afternoon too six in the evening--a total eclipse of the sun usually last a few minutes.

Then from the city came word at the cross of mass confusion: Something about ghosts, and a veil being torn in the Holy of Holies.

The Holy of Holies was a place where no one but the High Priest could go. Immediately death by the God of Israel awaited anyone but the High Priest who went into that room. The Romans never tested the Most Holy Place to see if it was fact or superstition.

The earthquake scared the wits out of the Romans; but they had experienced earthquakes before; this one would pass. Yet they noticed that even the rocks that sat on the ground broke in two; now that was a little different.

The news from the city temple was uninteresting to the Romans; they had gods of their own that wanted their mortal attention. But when they saw the souls leaving their resting places in the cemetery---that was another matter!

The Roman centurion declared aloud that Jesus was the Son of God. At that moment, perhaps, he may have regretted taking part in Jesus' crucifixion. Though he was only following the daily orders, this day would always be the worst day of his natural born life, an eerie story to tell his great grandchildren.

Little did the centurion know, the veil in the temple was torn to save sinners like him. The veil was ripped by the hand of God Almighty. The veil was thick and high; teams of oxen would've been needed to tear it in half. Through the veil, the crucified body of Jesus, whosoever would receive Him as Savior and Lord can safely enter into the Holy of Holies.

The enmity, the animosity which separated God from mankind was removed; the reconciliation needed to put our hand in God's hand so we can walk in agreement, Covenant, was established by the New Testament signed and sealed in the precious blood of Jesus.

What took place above ground was only the manifestation in the Physical Realm of Christ's victory. There remained issues to be settled beneath the earth. Satan had to be dealt with concerning Sheol. Jesus wouldn't rest until His people had rest.

> "Wherefore He said, When He ascended up on high, He led captivity captive, and gave gifts unto men. (Now that He ascended, what is it that He also descended first into the lower parts of the earth? He that descended is the same also that ascended up far above all heavens, that He might fill all things)" (Eph. 4:8-10).

When Jesus of Nazareth died upon the cross, His entire Person became a sin offering. Once He became spiritually dead because of the curse of sin attached to crucifixion, then physically dead, like Adam after he sinned, Jesus fulfilled the requirements to become interned, a legal resident of Sheol. So Immediately after His death on the cross, He arrived at Sheol:

Perhaps the demons applauded because they swore on the name of their master that the powers of darkness would one day quench and overpower the Light; they believed the day had come when Satan gained enough momentum and power to ascend back into Heaven and take what was rightfully his, and they would again govern with him the entire Physical Realm.

The Principalities, Powers, Rulers of the Darkness, Prince Spirits and Governors of the atmospheric heavens, celebrated the triumph over the descendants of Adam; it's likely they planned to increase the terror and torment of the Human race with sicknesses, diseases, poverty, calamity and horrible deaths.

But suddenly the decree of the Father went forth: "My Son, arise!" The Resurrection Anointing rushed into Sheol, found Jesus and raised Him from the dead! It was God's plan for Jesus Christ to die for our sin, cross over into the dimension into Sheol, and be raised from the dead.

Satan, the principalities, rulers and powers didn't know that God was capable of operating in their dominion; they *assumed* since they couldn't ascend into Heaven, that God couldn't descend into Sheol as a Human resident.

The reason why Jesus descended was to free the captives, those who were prisoners of the war between good and evil; from Adam too Christ, Sheol received the dead. "For to this end Christ both died, and rose, and revived, that He might be Lord both of the dead and living" (Romans 14:9).

Perhaps, when the Resurrection Anointing entered Sheol, the Spirit of God sounded like it did on the day of Pentecost (Acts 2:2). When the Life of God entered Jesus Christ, it was like a nuclear blast detonated in the heart of Sheol. The Resurrection Anointing conformed those who believed in Him into His image, preparing them for the journey and permanent residence in Heaven. The ground above shook. Jesus released many of the saints. They ascended out the ground and went into Jerusalem to declare the victory of the Lord Jesus Christ over Satan.

Christ descended to declare through the church His authority over the demonic powers, and His legal right as the Kinsmen Redeemer (Numbers 27:8-11) of Man, by Himself being the Son of man, a member of the human race. Jesus Christ exercised His authority, "to raise up the name of the dead upon his inheritance" (Ruth 4:3-5); not only on earth but in Sheol too.

Jesus Christ: "Who is the image of the invisible God, the firstborn of every creature: For by Him were all things created, that are in Heaven, and that are in earth, visible and invisible, whether they be thrones, or dominions, or principalities, or powers: all things were created by Him, and for Him" (Colossians 1:15,16).

Christ was destined to conquer Satan: "For in Him dwells all the fullness of the Godhead bodily. And having spoiled principalities and powers, He made a show of them openly, triumphing over them in it" (Colossians 2:9,15).

Christ always had authority over the demonic powers; the problem was recruiting faithful people willing to stand in the gap between Him and the land; Christ sought disgruntled people, so tired of being oppressed by the Devil to do something about him. Once He established His Covenant, He obtained the legal right to assist in taking back what the Devil stole from Adam and his descendants.

As our Kinsmen Redeemer, having the legal right of redemption of a purchased possession--those sold into the slavery of sin by Adam-- Jesus Christ purchased mankind with His own blood!

> "By which He preached unto the spirits in prison; which sometimes were disobedient, when once the longsuffering of God waited in the days of Noah..." (1 Peter 3:19).

The message Jesus preached in Sheol wasn't any different than the one He preached in Palestine: "The Spirit of the Lord is upon Me" was the foundation of His sermon. He preached and the demonic powers couldn't stop Him.

For three days and nights Jesus was separated from His physical body as it lay cold, wrapped in grave clothes and saturated with a hundred pounds of Spikenard; the wrapping was like a perfumed concrete cast.

Jesus preached what may have been decades in Sheol, considering the absence of time in the spirit realm. It was necessary that Jesus preach to the captives: "For this cause was the gospel preached also to them that are dead, that they might be judged according to men in the flesh, but live according to God in the Spirit" (1 Peter 4:6).

Faith is the standard by which people are saved; Faith is the trusting in and relying on the Gospel of Jesus Christ; there's no other standard. Everyone is judged by the Word of God--whether in or out of the grave. "For we must all appear before the judgment seat of Christ; that every one receive the things done in his body, according to that he has done, whether it be good or bad" (2 Corinthians 5:10). Those who accept the gospel are most fortunate.

The day following the crucifixion, the chief priests and Pharisees came to Pilate, "Saying, Sir, we remember that that deceiver said, while He was yet alive, After three days I will rise again. Command therefore that the sepulcher be made sure until the third day, lest His disciples come by night, and steal Him away, and say unto the people, He is risen from the dead: so THE LAST ERROR SHALL BE WORST THEN THE FIRST" (Matthew 27:63,64).

These men didn't know when to quit! Their admission of error and guilt was obvious to Pilate. He had dealt with this lot on several occasions. He knew they were covering up the killing of one of their own prophets.

Pilate had married a Jewess. He knew of their customs: How the Jews had exiled or killed every prophet the God of Israel sent. Now, they were behaving like criminals who were only sorry they got caught.

Nevertheless, to get them out of his face, Pilate dispatched guards to secure the sepulcher. The guards placed a large stone at the opening and secured it with a Roman Seal. If the stone was tampered with the seal would break.

The next morning, the first day of the week, there was an earthquake. The spiritually resurrected Jesus of Nazareth reentered His dead body. Suddenly, in the twinkle of an eye, His physical body transformed into a glorified body. The Resurrection Anointing was so powerful it scorched the grave-clothes and made an imprint on His face and body. The Lord Jesus Christ got up and escorted the Sheol captives to Heaven. Then an angel descended from Heaven and rolled the stone from the mouth of the sepulcher and sat on it.

The two Marys came to visit and saw the angel. The angel said to the women, "Fear not you; for I know that you seek Jesus, which was crucified. He is not here: for He is risen, as He said, see the place where the Lord lay" (Matthew 28:5,6).

We serve a risen Savior; the founders of the world religions are all dead, and if we would visit their burial places, resume them, we would discover their bones; certainly, sin and death swallowed them up and Hell became their eternal home. They weren't protected by their religions and failed to receive the Mystery of Christ in them.

"He is not here" is the testimony, authentication of the overcoming of death by Jesus Christ; for if He were an impostor, God wouldn't have raised Him from the dead.

The resurrection of our Lord is an eternal truth recorded in the archive of Heaven. God, Himself, has taken the witness stand and testified that He raised Jesus Christ from the dead.

"For there are three that bear record in heaven, the Father the Word, and the Holy Ghost: and these three are one. And there are three that bear witness in earth, the Spirit, and the water, and the blood: and these three agree in one. If we receive the witness of men, the witness of God is greater; for this is the witness of God which He has testified of His Son. He that believes on the Son of God has the witness in himself: he that believes not God has made Him a liar; because he believes not the record that God gave of His Son" (1 John 5:7-10). "And as they went to tell His disciples, behold, Jesus met them, saying, All hail. Then said Jesus unto them, Be not afraid: go tell My brethren that they go into Galilee, and there shall they see Me" (Matthew 28:9,10).

Jesus proved that He had risen from the dead. He was recognized and communicated with over five hundred people. He's the first fruit of them that slept, having become the first to resurrect from Adamic Death. Jesus is alive!

The Sanhedrin Council did all they could to keep the Word of the Lord Jesus Christ from coming to pass. "So the last error shall be worse than the first," was their admission of guilt in forwarding false accusations to the Governor concerning Jesus of Nazareth.

Then the religious leaders assembled to unleash a new plan. They gave a large sum of money to the soldiers who guarded the tomb. They told the soldiers to lie and say His disciples stole the dead body of Jesus. And when the Governor hears about it, the leaders would "persuade him" not to punish the soldiers (v.12-15).

Nevertheless, Jesus showed Himself alive and glorified on the road to a village called Emmaus. He talked with two Believers: One of them was named Cleopas. Jesus discussed the Scriptures with them, how it was written that Christ would suffer and die at the hands of sinners. At first they didn't recognize Him. But after He prayed there was no doubt in their minds--no one can pray as fervent as Jesus! Then, He vanished out of their sight.

All the men could say was, "Did not our hearts burn within us, while He talked with us by the way, and while He opened to us the scriptures? (Luke 24:32).   The passionate Savior touched their hearts with the Anointed Word: It was like fire shut up in their bones.

Later, the disciples were hiding in a room. They were afraid the religious leaders would have them arrested, tried and crucified like Jesus. The door was locked. Suddenly, Jesus stood in the midst of them. He said, "Peace be unto you. But they were terrified and frightened, and supposed that they had seen a spirit"(v.36,37).

After realizing who He was, they rejoiced in the Resurrection and the Life. Jesus showed them his nail scared hands and His wounded side. Then Jesus breathed on them and they received the Holy Ghost (John 20:22).

When the disciples went to the tomb and saw the grave clothes they should have stopped to listen: Those grave clothes symbolically preached a sermon! As actions speak louder than words, so that empty tomb echoed and amplified the Gospel message preached by the empty grave clothes. Those grave clothes preached the binding up of the broken hearted, liberty to the captives, the opening of the prison to them that are bound by sicknesses, diseases, addictions, poverty, sin and death. The grave clothes testified to the tearing down of Satan's wicked kingdom, and the advancement of the Kingdom of God on earth.

Thomas and the other disciples did well when Jesus was physically among them; they fell into doubt when He was physically taken away. Thomas thought that "seeing is believing", but Biblical Faith is believing before seeing what's promised in the Word.

Thomas wasn't commended for his acceptance of the Resurrection, but was rebuked for his faithlessness, worldly intellect that must see with the natural eyes before believing; faith is seeing with the eyes of the Human spirit empowered by the Presence of the Holy Spirit, Christ in you.

Take Abraham for example: "And Abram said, LORD God, what will You give me, *seeing* I go childless..." (Genesis 15:2). His seeing with the physical eyes the circumstances that stood in the way of him receiving the Promise of Isaac. The Holy Ghost would make it possible.

Now Mary: "Then said Mary unto the angel, How shall this be, *seeing* I know not a man? And the angel answered and said unto her, The Holy Ghost shall come upon thee, and the power of the highest shall overshadow thee: therefore that holy thing which shall be born of thee shall be called the Son of God" (Luke 1:34,35).

Mary was a young virgin when the angel Gabriel visited her. She knew about life, that it takes a male and a female to create a baby; yet, "seeing" she wasn't having a sexual relationship with a man, she was perplexed in her natural thinking.

Until she believed Gabriel's report, nothing could be done. Her "seeing" in the natural prevented God from doing the supernatural. Mary wasn't doubting the Messenger or the message, but was lacking in understanding. When she understood that God was going to perform a miracle in her life, she rejoiced and said, "Behold, the handmade of the Lord; be it unto me according to thy word"(v.38). Then Gabriel departed from her; the Holy Ghost entered and impregnated her, and she brought forth God's and her First Born Son. (Adam was created from the ground, but Jesus born of a woman.)

The Word states the one who is blessed is the one who hasn't seen yet believes in the Word, Name, and Blood of Jesus Christ.

Before Jesus left His disciples He said, "And these signs shall follow them that believe; in My Name shall they cast out devils; they shall speak with new tongues...They shall lay hands on the sick, and they shall recover" (Mark 16:17,18). "And, behold, I send the

PROMISE OF MY FATHER UPON YOU: but tarry ye in the city of Jerusalem, until ye be endued with power from on High" (Luke 24:49).

Notes

CHAPTER FOUR
JESUS IS ALIVE

In the previous chapters, we explored the human side of Jesus of Nazareth, the Messenger and the Gospel message, including His death, burial, and resurrection. We have also touched the depths of who Christ is. Now we must know Him as the resurrected Jesus, the glorified awesome Spirit Being with infinite authority--He who was once a mere man was "conformed" into Christ, and given a Name above all other names.

Everything He voluntarily set aside in becoming the Son of Man (a Human Being), He received back, and more--the Church--which is His body, the "many sons of glory produced from a single but awesome Seed.

The risen Savior is who we must "progressively become more deeply and intimately acquainted" with, and "come to know the power out-flowing from His Resurrection." This power exerts "Himself" over Believers.

Again, genuine Faith is the key; without Faith in the finished work of the cross, the revelation in our spirit that Christ actually arose from the dead, we can't walk in the newness of the resurrected life.

Remember, God testified as a witness that He raised Jesus of Nazareth from the dead. The glorified Lord Jesus Christ was seated at the right hand of God, where He continuously ministers as High Priest, and makes intercession for the Saints of God.

He's our High Priest, who after Resurrection ascended into Heaven, then entered into the "original" Eternal Temple where exist the Holy of Holies. Then as the Lamb of God, He poured upon the Mercy Seat His own Blood as an Atonement for our sins, thus fulfilling the Word: The Lamb slain before the foundation of the world.

He reigns as Savior and Lord. He wants to reign as Savior and Lord within our spirit too. Christ can rule not only Heaven, but the Earth through our hearts.

We must strive to lay hold of Christ within and know Him as Who we will become; as He is, we shall be also. Isn't that worth pursuing?

In the Old Testament it was written in Isaiah 64:4 "For since the beginning of the world men have not heard, nor perceived by the ear, neither has the eye seen, 0 God, beside You, what He has prepared for him that waits for Him."

But that has all changed since Jesus Christ, the Messiah has come and opened up the windows of Heaven: "But God hath revealed them unto us by His Spirit; for the Spirit searches all things, yeah, the deep things of God" (1 Cor. 2.10).

Now it's possible for us to perceive and know the Person of God. This divine wisdom and knowledge is searched out by the Holy Spirit and deposited, downloaded into our spirit. We perceive and therefore know the deep things of God; His character and personality, through our spiritual facility called intuition ---divine connection into the omniscience of God.

We can know the Triune Godhead: The Holy Spirit is the Spirit of the Father and the Spirit of Christ. Since the Holy Spirit indwells Believers, we're included in another Mystery: The Triune Godhead as: Father/Son-Church/Holy Spirit. What a blessing! Yes, the Church is "In Him," as He is "In Us."

A great division arose in the early years of the Church. False prophets and teachers secretly crept in and taught that Christ didn't resurrect from the dead. They also taught that works, circumcision and the traditions of the Mosaic Law, was essential to Salvation.

Their motives were to "control" the freedom the Christians had, and bring them back under Mosaic jurisdiction, the Law and the Sanhedrin Council. The temple treasury lost money because Christians no longer were a part of it.

But Jesus Christ fulfilled the obligation, the spiritual, legal and moral requirements of the Law; to return Christians to bondage was the goal of the religious spirits, who crept in to "bewitch" the body of Christ. These spirits established the world religions and uses them to combat Christianity. The evil spirits also seek to modify Christianity to change it into a more compromising or "user friendly" Gospel, thus perverting it and thus rendering the Word of God of no effect:
Powerless to Heal, Deliver, Save or manifest Miracles.

Today, Special Interest Groups lobby to change the U.S. Constitution to accommodate what the majority of people really want: To live immoral, non-Christian lives. Their fighting for their inalienable, undeniable free-will right to go to Hell.

Paul told the Christians, "But though we, or an angel from heaven, preach any other gospel unto you than that which we have preached unto you, let him be accursed" (Galatians 1:8,9).

Without the resurrection of Jesus Christ there is no gospel, no good news, no peace with God, and therefore no Salvation obtained: Everyone is lost--and it's the bad news gospel.

The Apostle Paul's argument was not only to the early church but the modern church: Salvation depends on the truth that Jesus died on the cross for our sins, that He arose from the dead by the Commandment of God, which even the old prophets foretold.

If our hope was only in this life--- like the religions---we're of all people most miserable! We know that through Adam sin and death came into the world; so through Christ, the second Adam, came the Divine Resurrection.

> "And so it is written, The first man, Adam was made a living soul; the last Adam was made a quickening Spirit" (1 Cor. 15:45).

Today, there are people who refuse to believe in the Resurrection of Jesus Christ. People find it easy to believe that He lived and died, but to admit that He accomplished the Atonement for the sins of Mankind (only for those who believe in Him, not a blanket of forgiveness), and arose from the dead, is too much; and there are those who confess with their head (and go to church) but don't believe in their heart that Jesus is Lord, who feel guilty for not serving Him.

Being convinced and convicted of the truth, they would be obligated to worship Him--and this doesn't fit into their plans of self worship and continuing in the darkness of sin.

Other than Christianity, no other path, philosophy or religion has claimed that their founder is God, the Son of God, Christ or any such Deity; their founders never claimed to be a Sacrifice.

In fact, most religions minimize the reality and consequences of sin in order to attract followers. Religion pushes the need for good works as the way to please God and enter Heaven at the end of days. They sidestep the bare essential, the necessity of Faith in Jesus Christ.

Bloodless religion (not fanatics blowing themselves up and killing innocent people in the name of their religion) adhere to rituals, traditions, programs, legalism, brainwashing and "politically correct" morality, and insist they're equal to the followers of Christ. Many claim to have a personal relationship with God: Nay--they haven't a clue who God is! Misguided souls regard Jesus Christ as only a prophet, a good person; that Christianity is the "white man's religion." These same people proclaim Holy Wars, sanction racial hatred, destruction and murder; these are mere cults.

The lost deny the existence of God in favor of science and evolution. The legalist and politicians submit bills and resolutions to separate the church from the government. They desire to "erase" the Christian language and values from all official documents including the United States Constitution, and ban biblical teachings and prayer out of public schools.

Unknowingly, they represent the powers of darkness,(in the case of witches and warlocks, they knowingly operate in the psychic arts.) they secretly want to keep the metal detectors, policemen, drugs, guns, violence, murder, gangs, rapes, and witchcraft in the schools.

They hate Christ; in their hearts they say, "Let His blood be on us and on our children!" So they're more than willing to sacrifice the children rather than let His Presence into the schools. They're afraid the children will receive Christ and bring Him home!

False prophets and teachers are still among us; they never left, but passed their misinformation down through the generations. They work to stop the Resurrection Anointing of Jesus Christ from restoring the souls and renewing the minds of mankind. The Enemy of the resurrection promotes lawlessness, so his followers can live whatever perverse, depraved and indifferent lives they please. They try to persuade us through legislation, logic, science and civil liberty organizations that God and the local churches should be subject to Federal and State Constitutional Laws, and what the majority of the people want; and since there are more non-Christians and carnal (religious) Christians, they achieve their goals; the anti-Christ supports them.

It's shocking how many Christians don't have a problem with Gay Marriage or Abortion.

Then there are those who believe that God "feels" like they do. He's so pitiful and weak that He can't bring Himself to send anyone to Hell; He would rather fill Heaven with unrepentant murders, rapist, robbers, gangsters and liars than punish them for their sins; under this type of doctrine, what incentive is there to live a good moral life, if we all eventually end up at the same place? This is called the "Inclusion Doctrine."

If that was true Heaven would be the wildest continuous abode of wickedness ever imagined; the holy angels would be more like U.S. Marshals or Military Police! Heaven wouldn't be a place of Eternal Rest, Love, Joy, Peace and Tranquility; people who don't Worship and Praise Jesus on the earth, would be miserable in Heaven where EVERYONE praises Him. Heaven would become Hell to those who despise Jesus.

Still others teach that whatever laws men pass are accepted without question by God.

One bunch of idiots state that aliens from outer space populated the earth, then left us to simmer in our own gravy; others say creation is finished and God departed for parts unknown --but before He left He wrote a short note, saying, "Just do what you think is right in your own eyes!" So the Chancellor of Germany, Adolf Hitler persuaded his people to exterminated millions of Jews and Gypsies; because it was the right thing to do in his own eyes!

Human History is loaded with examples of what happens when leaders or just ordinary people do what they believe is right in their own eyes: In more modern times, Saddam Husain used poisonous gas on the Kurds; he too thought it was right in his own eyes; as did the Southern slave owners and modern day drug and human traffickers. Today its mass shootings in our schools and other places; if life without God, we would destroy ourselves and be right in our own eyes while accomplishing it!

Many claim God is dead, and man is the center of existence, that Christianity is a manmade religion: They believe that Man made God, not God made Man. It's the spirit of death working in the hearts of the false teachers, the anti-Christ of this generation.

Christ in you, the Mystery will triumph. The last enemy that shall be destroyed is death--and Satan knows it, but is powerless to do anything about it. Yes, God has his number, the date and time of Satan's destruction!

Everywhere we explore in the Word of God are hidden Mysteries, treasures hidden in the depths of the Ocean of Love and Mercy which is God. There's such depth to Christ that we could live several lifetimes and but touch the surface of who He is. So the sooner we get started the better!

We shall not die but live, and declare the Name of the Lord. We shall not die and be forever lost, but transformed, evolved from one level and dimension of consciousness to a higher level of dimension and consciousness.

We confessed our sins and confessed our Faith in the Word and in Jesus Christ. The Holy Spirit of Christ immediately responded and resurrected our spiritually dead Human spirit; then, in the process of time, He will restore our soul and renew our mind. This process is called Sanctification.

When our spirit was indwelled by Christ, our soul/mind and physical body remained un-regenerated; it's the mission of the Spirit of God to gradually conform us into the image of Jesus Christ; At the moment of Salvation, our spirit was immediately transformed--but our soul/mind wasn't immediately transformed.

If we should physically die or Jesus Christ returns before the work of the Holy Spirit is done in our life, Sanctification will be completed; the soul will be immediately restored to a Christ-like image, the mind will be renewed to Christ-like thoughts, and the physical body will be transformed from mortality to immortality.

This natural body will become a super-natural body like the one Jesus Christ has today (and after His Calvary resurrection). This body corresponds with the heavenly realm.

The completion of Sanctification is the redemption of our entire person; the completion of Salvation is called Glorification.

Glorification Day or Second Coming, is the day when Jesus returns. A trumpet will sound, and death will be swallowed up in victory. No longer will the sting of death exercise its power over our soul through our abuse of God's laws. Free at last! Free at last!

The third type of death is pronounced at the Great White Throne Judgment where Jesus Christ, the Righteous Judge resides on the throne and judges the unsaved whose names aren't written in the Lamb's Book of Life.

The wicked dead are those who refused to accept Jesus as their Savior and Lord. Sins aren't discussed here; only one sin, and that's failure to accept the Lord, to allow Him to justify (declare not guilty, acquit) them by the Law of Faith.

Everyone who receives the White Throne Judgment is cast into the Lake of Fire (Revelations 20:15). When the last enemy, Satan is judged, he will also be cast into the Lake of Fire.

In these uncertain times, death brings such a sting; the sting, the pain of losing a loved one to accident, violence, disease or old age. The pain can become as a sharp knife being twisted into the pit of the stomach.

Mourning, lamentation, tears, grief and loneliness are part of death's legacy. Death's desire is to torture us into questioning the motives of God. This will lead to doubt, insecurity and depression. When we know the deceased suffered through a prolonged decline and then death comes, we reason that death wasn't such a bad thing; it brought relief.

But death to the unsaved is always a Human tragedy! Death isn't a prescription, an escape vehicle or mechanism for the unsaved; Salvation, Spiritual Healing and Deliverance is available for the asking, in Him.

God is on Earth in the form of the Holy Spirit; but in Hell, He's not there. Only the hot blue flames of a lake of fire and brimstone awaits the unsaved. Blue flame is extremely hot, and Hell is extremely dark because blue flame doesn't create much visibility. There's no escape, no hope!

The eternally lost receive a funeral but the Saved receive a Home Going. The redeemed of the Lord aren't dead, but live on in a higher dimension and state of consciousness.

Christians shouldn't mourn in an unhealthy manner over those who have departed in Christ. We shouldn't mourn as those who have no hope beyond the grave. We believe (trust in, rely on) the Word of God; so even as Christ was raised from the dead, our brothers and sisters who sleep (not are dead) in Him will be escorted over into the unseen yet lively realm of Righteousness, Peace and Joy.

We're also comforted in knowing that when we get there our relatives and friends who left before us, those who ARE IN CHRIST, have no advantage or disadvantage because they or we arrived at different times;

"For a thousand years in Thy sight are but as yesterday when it is past, and as a watch in the night" (Psalms 90:4). There's no biblical evidence that time in the spirit realms equals the same in the Physical Realm.

It may appear to all Mankind that we cross over at the same moment. Spirit realms like Sheol, Heaven, or Hell are realms where the terms "eternity," "eternal," and "forever" are used as a common measurement of time.

On Glorification Day the trumpet will sound. The Lord Jesus Christ will descend from the clouds and those who sleep in Christ will come out of their graves, and the sea shall give up its dead to the Lord Christ. Then we who are journeying in the Physical Realm will simultaneously be caught up into the clouds to forever be with the Lord.

Glorification Day isn't far off; but the evangelism of the entire world must come first. Then the Blessed Hope, the Kinsmen Redeemer will return for His purchased possession. Jesus is alive: Death has lost its victory and the grave has been denied. Jesus lives forever!

AN AWESOME SPIRIT BEING

The Mystery of Christ is so deep. When we consider that Jesus was both God and man, the Son of God and the Son of Man, an attempt to separate the two for the sake of understanding, we discover a paradox, and that too is the Mystery.

It is extraordinary that Jesus of Nazareth had the Holy Spirit, Human Spirit, Human Soul, and Human Body in one mortal package. This would be necessary to be totally Human and Divine; Christ the Word resident within Him, was in His Human spirit; And so now Christians are also four-part New Creatures: Holy Spirit, Human Spirit, Human

Human Soul, and Human Physical Body; unsaved people are only three-part.

Jesus is an awesome Spirit Being. Yet, Jesus said the reason why He could do such miracles was not because He's God, but that He was Anointed by the Holy Spirit to do them.

Before His baptism in the Holy Spirit, Jesus of Nazareth, a man predestined to be the Lord, had the potential of being our Savior, but could choose not to sacrifice Himself, and thereby become like the rest of us---sinners.

Of Course the Holy Spirit within Jesus of Nazareth was already the Lord God, but His Soul, Mind and Physical Body had to be changed into the image of God. Jesus had personality shaped from His parents. God also gave Him revelation, and used Jesus' environment and social relationships to teach Him obedience. He had individuality and opinions, which He chose not to exalt. Instead, He exalted the Father, and became the Lamb of God.

This shouldn't surprise us, seeing we're His spiritual descendents; we're earthen vessels indwelled by the Holy Spirit. This alone gives us the potential to do great and mighty works for the kingdom of God. We too are awesome spirit beings with infinite potential.

And this was the purpose of His incarnation: To raise up the name of the dead--our name--upon our inheritance. He came to raise all the Lazarus' from the dead.

In the Physical Realm, binding and loosing authority was conferred upon the Church, the children of God. The authority and Spirit power to put demons and their works to flight was in our Covenant. Whatever God doesn't permit in Heaven because it's improper and unlawful, we don't have to allow on earth either!

Even the spiritual wickedness, the princes who rule the lower heavens are made ineffective by Christ, in response to our prayers and Christian authority to administer the New Testament Covenant.

It's the Physical Realm where the binding and loosing is first initiated, not in Heaven. It's in the Physical Realm where the Church must come into unity--agreement, harmony, a symphony—with the Church at the throne of God. The Physical Body of Christ must agree with the Spiritual Body of Christ in Heaven, before the

Holy Spirit will change things down here; it's God's will.

This is where we as Christians miss the mark: We spend a lot of time not praying--but begging for God to do what He already gave us authority to do. When the Church was an infant and needed a lot of help, He was there to carry her; now the Church is over two thousand years old, she should be walking with Him. The Church should be strong and ruling the world; but the world is ruling the Church-- binding and loosing us!

He said, "Behold, I give you power to tread on serpents and scorpions, and over ALL THE POWER OF THE ENEMY; and nothing shall by any means hurt you" (Luke 9:19). These are the signs that follow them that believe; these aren't just signs for the Ministry Gifts: Apostles, prophets, evangelists, pastors, or teachers--but signs and wonders that follow ANY believer in Christ Jesus.

True, the Ministry Gifts have received delegated Leadership An- ointing and a greater measure of the Holy Spirit; but all Believers, are anointed by the Holy Spirit.

The Holy Spirit flows through Christ's Body, bringing it into unity with Himself. The Word of God, Name of Jesus, and Blood of Jesus are integrated into the Covenant of Blessing.

Seeing we have in us the consummation of the Covenant, Christ in us, and have submitted to God and resisted the Devil, we can---in the Name of Jesus---command the spirit of sickness to leave!

Jesus stated as Believers in Him we have the same authority on earth as we have in Heaven. The key to victory is knowing and putting into practice the scriptures, knowing Whose and who we are. Our very words have Spirit power when Faith is added to them.

We must "say" to the mountains in our life--be thou removed! The- se mountains may be sickness, poverty, depression or oppression of the Devil; they may be addictions, fears, or marital problems; they could even be everyday stress from working and raising a family.

Whenever the Holy Spirit is needed, we can speak Him into our situation. We can also run demons out of our life or the lives of those we pray for. By speaking the Word of Faith, we confer blessings to come upon and overtake those we pray for.

But the enemy of Faith is doubt. We must not doubt in our heart that God is ready, willing and able to meet our needs. In short, we must have FAITH IN GOD AND THE FAITH OF GOD.

God has great Faith because He is the Author of Faith. God believes--adheres to, trust in, and relies on--His words; we must also apply this biblical definition and believe in our own Spirit-inspired words in order to manifest them; then we can have whatsoever we say.

As awesome spirit beings, God has given us exceedingly great and precious Promises. When Jesus walked the earth as the Son of man, He performed thousands of healings, miracles, signs and wonders.

At great length He described the provisions, guarantees and oaths of the New Testament Covenant. He graciously spoke to the crowd about the Promise of the Father, that He would return to the Father. He was the kernel of wheat that would fall to the earth and die.

Then He would send back the Comforter to forever abide with His followers. For John truly baptized with water; but YOU SHALL BE BAPTIZED WITH THE HOLY GHOST not many days hence" Then He continued and said, "But you SHALL RECEIVE POWER, after that the Holy Ghost is come upon you; and you shall be witnesses unto Me..." (Acts 1:5,).

When the Lord Jesus Christ arose from the dead, He ascended into Heaven with the captives of Sheol. From the throne of God He sent back to the Physical Realm the Promise of the Father which is the Holy Spirit. With the arrival of the Holy Spirit came the authority and endowment of power for all Believers to become like Christ. The Resurrection Anointing to destroy yokes surged through the Body of Christ in the Physical Realm.

The Church was first established at the throne of God, then on the day of Pentecost, it was established in the Physical Realm.

Jesus also sent back the Leadership Anointing, the Ministry Gifts: "And He gave some, Apostles; some, Prophets; and some, Evangelists; and some, Pastors; and some, Teachers; For the perfecting of the saints, for the work of the ministry, for the edifying of the body of Christ: Till WE ALL COME IN THE UNITY OF THE FAITH, and of the knowledge of the Son of God, unto a perfect (complete) man, unto the MEASURE OF THE STATUE OF THE FULLNESS OF CHRIST" (Ephesians 4:11-13).

Not only did God anoint Jesus Christ with the Holy Ghost and with power, but Jesus Christ became the One who Baptizes us in the Holy Spirit!

He has also placed in the Church anointed people to channel His Blessing into the congregation. He did this to exhort, instruct, correct, rebuke, and expose the hidden wisdom and knowledge in the heart of God; even the hidden Mysteries and Treasures not obvious to the natural mind, are daily being revealed to those who possess the Ministry Gifts.

The Holy Spirit is given through Grace--unmerited favor; Salvation is received in response to repentance of sins and confession of Faith in Jesus Christ. The authority and privilege to be called Children of God is based upon voluntarily receiving the Holy Spirit; the Baptism in the Holy Spirit, the second work of grace, is also received by Faith.

The Holy Spirit, a living Person walks among us seeking those who have been called and predestined to Salvation. He woos us to freely accept Him so He can enter our spirit and make His residence there. Because the Holy Spirit is God, He has the authority to forgive sins and to save. The ability to make confession of sins and confession of Faith in Jesus Christ comes from the wooing in our heart by the Holy Spirit. He brings us to repentance.

Without the Holy Spirit to strengthen us, we cannot live what we confess with our mouth. Though we may sincerely believe what we have decided in our heart, we cannot perform or live the Christian lifestyle without the help of the Holy Spirit. Through this, we become awesome spirit beings with infinite potential.

> "Then Samuel took the horn of oil, and anointed him in the midst of his brethren, "and the Spirit of the Lord came upon David from that day forward" (1 Sam.16:13).

David became one of several awesome spirit beings in the Old Testament. In the above verse, he was anointed King of Israel. God's decision to anoint David king wasn't based on who David was, but God looked upon David's humble respect and disposition towards His Name. Then God anointed David to be captain over His inheritance, and a new creation, a man after God's own heart.

Though David was anointed and loved God, he wasn't sinless; he made plenty of mistakes; for all have sinned and missed the mark.

Moreover, David had a personal relationship with God. David claimed his Covenant right and cleaved to it with his very life; God in return claimed His Covenant right, and wouldn't leave David or forsake him.

David became a type of Christ; he was anointed by the Holy Spirit as king of Israel. David was also a priest of a different order and rank than the Leviticus Order. Therefore, David had the authority to confer blessings upon the people.

God used Samuel to anoint David. Samuel stood in the offices of Judge (like a king), High Priest, and Prophet. Samuel was of the sons of Aaron; Aaron was Moses' brother, who was ordained the first High Priest, whose descendents brought forth all the Mosaic High Priests. So, Samuel was of the tribe of Levi, as were the priests who carried the Ark of the Covenant.

Samuel died; King Saul murdered the next High Priest for helping David to escape (1 Samuel 22:18. Now, we see David from the Tribe of Judah--not Levi--offered sacrifices and standing in the holy Office of High Priest.

When King Saul, the first King of Israel offered sacrifice to God as David had done, Saul was rebuked: "And Samuel stated, Has the LORD as great delight in burnt offerings and sacrifices, as in obeying the voice of the LORD? Behold, to obey is better than sacrifice, and to hearken then the fat of rams. For rebellion is as the sin of witchcraft, and stubbornness is as iniquity and idolatry. Because you have rejected the Word of the LORD, He has also rejected you from being king" (1 Samuel 15:22,23).

David knew the reason for Saul's downfall; he knew the consequences of assuming authority that wasn't delegated to him. But David received revelation from the LORD.

Because of this, he had permission to minister in the Office of High Priest, in that he was the first of a new order of King-Priest; in which generations later the Lion of the Tribe of Judah, Jesus Christ, the Messiah, the Anointed One would walk the Earth.

The ephod was worn by the priests. It was a sleeveless linen vest. And because David was a priest, he wore an ephod under his robe. He was the spiritual owner of this garment because in God's wisdom he was ordained a priest under a different tabernacle, called the Tabernacle of David. The Tabernacle of David was Faith-based. It was a breathtaking new Praise and Worship Order. David directed, as a Worship Leader leads the congregation---and offered the sacrifices while standing in the Office of High Priest.

When David was being hunted by Saul, he hid in a city. Word came that King Saul planned to besiege the city. Immediately, David sent for the ephod. Why would he send for a linen garment that wasn't his? Or why would he need the ephod to talk with God?

The ephod was a linen garment that all the priests wore. But there were two types of ephods: The priests wore a plain linen ephod, but the High Priest's ephod was special: It was brightly colored and embroidered; it had a bib-like breastplate with gold shoulder straps, with twelve gemstones representing each Tribe.

In the pouch was the Urim and the Thummim (Exodus 28:30), two small objects used to determine God's will concerning the nation. God spoke through the High Priest's ephod-oracle. This was what David sent after; he was God's New Creation, an awesome spirit being with infinite potential.

> "Therefore, if any man be in Christ, he is a new creature: old things are passed away; behold, all things are become new" (2 Corinthians 5:17).

David wasn't a New Creature by New Testament standards, but definitely by Old Testament standards; he didn't have Christ within, but Christ upon him, who spoke to him through the Urim and the Thummim Oracles.

We discover that not only was David the King of Israel, he was a priest--even a High Priest--and a Prophet. David, like Samuel, held several Offices; he also had many gifts (he wrote many of the Psalms) and talents which made him a man after God's own heart; he had powerful leadership and prophetic dispensations of the Holy Spirit, which set him apart from the other kings, prophets, priests, and worshippers of God.

David was a chosen vessel, an example of how God can change an ordinary man into an extraordinary man. Though David was a skillful warrior and wise king, the praise and worship belonged exclusively to the Lord, who Covenant with him, conformed and transformed David from a shy shepherd boy into a type of Christ.

It's God who causes us to triumph. He seats us in heavenly places with Himself. We're saved by grace through faith in Him. We're justified, sanctified and partakers of His divine nature.

Having been redeemed from the curse of the Mosaic Law, and delivered from the powers of darkness, we're led by the Spirit of the Son.

> "And from Jesus Christ, who is the faithful witness, and the first begotten of the dead, and the Prince of the kings of the earth. Unto Him that loved us, and washed us from our sins in His own blood. And bath MADE US KINGS AND PRIESTS UNTO GOD and His Father; to Him be glory and dominion forever and ever. Amen" Revelation 1:6).

The Apostle John wrote of the blessed, the redeemed of the Lord. All our needs are met by and through Jesus Christ. He's our High Priest, the Mediator between God and Man.

One day when the trials and tribulations in the physical are over, we'll sing a new song; it's a song that the heavenly angels can't sing-- because they weren't redeemed by the blood of Jesus. "And they sung a new song, saying, You are worthy to take the book, and to open the seals thereof: for You was slain, and have redeemed us to God by Your blood out of every kindred, and tongue, and people, and nation; And have MADE US 'UNTO GOD KINGS AND PRIESTS; and we shall reign on the earth" (Revelation 5:9,10).

We're kings and priests. Kings must have kingdoms, priests must have ministries: We reign and govern with Him in the Physical Realm, New Jerusalem, and in Heaven.

If we're to be good leaders and ministers in Heaven, we need to start practicing conformity to the example of Christ. This Physical Realm is God's classroom. As the righteousness of God in Christ, we must submit to the Holy Spirit and become an imitator of Christ.

"Blessed and holy is he that has part in the First Resurrection: on such the Second Death has no power, but THEY SHALL BE PRIESTS OF GOD and of Christ, and shall reign with Him a thousand years" (Rev.20:6). We're awesome spirit beings.

CHAPTER FIVE
PRAYER, PRAISE AND WORSHIP

When Prayer, Praise and Worship go up to the Throne of God, the blessings and manifestations of the Resurrection Anointing will fall upon those who offer it in Faith.

David was a man whose determined purpose was to know God. David knew the worth of spiritual sacrifice. He cleaved to them as the direct route to the Person of God. David freely offered to God the sacrifices of Praise and thanksgiving, the fruit of his lips giving thanks unto His holy Name.

David was a type, a good example of a common man being changed by the Goodness and Mercy of God. David's heart melted from the tender Mercy of God. God showed His unfailing Love by honoring His Covenant; David slew a lion, bear, Goliath the giant and the enemies of Israel by the strength he received from Jehovah, the God who makes Covenant.

Many times God spared David's life because David prayed; his enemies came one way but fled from him seven ways. One time David's enemies were so numerous and cunning--even his own men wanted to stone him--but David encouraged himself; he found strength and hope in the Lord God of his salvation. There were times when David honored the Lord with a spontaneous outbreak of praise and worship.

One may not think that a mighty man would weep; but David wept just thinking about the Goodness of the Lord. He wasn't concerned about who was watching. He wept in front of the notorious Mighty Men, because he wasn't ashamed; his hope was in the unseen not in himself, the valor or opinions of his men. David was God's favorite man on the earth.

By today's standards, David would be a fanatic. When Christians go all out and praise the Lord some Christians--the frozen chosen --- frown upon it. They say, "It don't take all that!"

It's understandable when the unsaved make such statements: They are spiritually dead. But lukewarm Christians feel threatened, embarrassed when we Praise with a loud and fervent voice.

Nevertheless, we must please God and not men; we cannot let unbelievers, religious people, or lukewarm Christians dictate how serious, personal or intimate we should be with our Lord. To be a Christian fanatic is good; all Christians should be sold out and uncompromising in the Faith. If this was so, the local churches would be all that God called them to be.

We should not wait until Thanksgiving Day to give thanks unto the Lord. God has done so much for us: He has given us Salvation, Deliverance, health, wealth and blessed us with His Presence, which includes the Fruit of the Spirit (Galatians 5:22,23).

He has answered our intercessory prayers for the healings and peace of our loved ones, and granted us the desires of our heart. Truly, He's worthy to be praised for all of His wonderful deeds. God's not asking for much--only that we should sing psalms, spiritual songs letting our heart rejoice before Him.

He remembered His Covenant, the oath He swore to Abraham, Who fulfilled it in Christ, so we may have Life and have it more abundantly. We praise Him for overseeing the safe deliveries of our newborn babies, and for watching over them each and every day. We thank Him for protection from obvious dangers, and the things we cannot see: The demonic spirits who harass and scheme to harm us. Jesus rebukes and dispatches warring angels to guard and protect us and those we pray for.

> 14 "And David danced before the LORD with all his might; and David was girded with a linen ephod. 16 Michal looked through the window, and saw David leaping and dancing before the LORD; and she despised him in her heart" 2 Samuel 6:14-16,(KJV).

Who can curse whom God has blessed? Michal, through her natural eyes, didn't see David as the humble servant of God but saw him through Satan's evil eyes: A man whom replaced Saul, her father as king, and the man who became king instead of one of her brothers or even distant relatives; plus she despised him because he embarrassed her by dancing wildly and acting a fool; what would her friends think? She would likely be laughed out of her "circle!"

She saw David as being strange, nothing like her father. This difference embarrassed her and made her extremely uncomfortable and conscious of her own social "image." Thus she accused him of exposing his "underwear" to Israel. To her, the ephod was common underwear.

But David, having thrown off his kingly apparel, had his priestly ephod underneath and wasn't naked or shamefully dressed. He was before God a man after His own heart! David leaped and danced in the Spirit; he was a sight to see.

The Children of Israel welcomed a change from the evil-hearted Saul. While Saul was pursuing David, Saul ordered Doeg to execute the High Priest, Aheimelech plus eighty-five priests who wore the linen ephod; Saul ordered the butchering of their families and destroyed their belongings (1 Samuel 22:18). (he did what was right in his own eyes!) Saul wasn't a man after God's own heart.

David and the Levites offered the sacrifices of glorious Praises and singing unto the Lord. The Lord was delighted; the Worship brought pleasure to Him, and He blessed David and Israel.

The Anointed are those who joyfully offer Praises to the Lord. And He who inhabits the Praises of His people will strengthen those who lift up holy hands to Him. The Word of God keeps our spirit encouraged and stirred up; giving praise is becoming of saints.

God has declared: "Saying, Touch not My Anointed, and do My prophets no harm" (Psalms 105:15.). Our Praises are eternal and precious in the sight of the Lord. Therefore, anyone who steals God's glory and Praise or vexes those who offer that sweet fragrance unto Him could find themselves being like Michal--cursed.

Strife against the true worshippers of God may be the reason why some well-meaning Christians are continuously struggling with health and financial burdens.

This is even said of Communion: "For he that eats and drinks unworthily, eats and drinks damnation to himself, NOT DISCERNING THE LORD"S BODY. For this cause MANY ARE WEAK AND SICK-LY AMONG YOU, AND MANY SLEEP (have died)" (1 Corinthians 11:29,30).

The Corinthian church was abundant with Spiritual Gifts, yet many suffered because they didn't discern the difference between what's holy, the things of God, from the profane, the things of the world. Communion may not seem like a form of worship but it is.

We become "conservative" when it comes to the true things of God

Jesus wasn't conservative, He was a radical, a trailblazer as nonreligious and nontraditional as the Father. Why are we trying to be conservative and religious concerning Praise and Worship?

Are we conserving our strength for self-interest? When we were unsaved, we ran hard for the Devil: Nothing stopped us--rain, snow, sleet, hail, or even gunfire--from getting to a party, dope house, or having sex with a "friend with benefits"!

Why, suddenly, are we conservative with our adoration? Have we become too proud, arrogant, or religious to look up to Heaven and give praise to Him who sits upon the throne and has kind intent towards us?

> "If My people, which are called by My Name, shall humble themselves, and pray, and seek my face, and turn from their wicked ways..." 2 Chron. 7:14 (KJV).

Solomon prayed an intense and emotional prayer as he dedicated the temple to the Name of the Lord, who dwelled between the Cherubims of Glory at the Mercy Seat. In response to the prayer, the fire of the Holy Ghost fell to Earth and consumed the offering.

Then the Glory of the Lord moved from the Holy of Holies as a thick cloud: The Glory Cloud was so intense the priests couldn't stand long enough to minister! The people humbled themselves, bowed their faces to the pavement and worshipped.

As the Lord chose the temple that King Solomon built as a "place to Myself for an house of sacrifice," we're now that place, that habitation of the Presence of God, that "house of sacrifice"; we're the living sacrifice who offers the sacrifices of Prayer, Praise and Worship which is our spiritual duty.

As sacrificial temples filled with the Presence of God, the Resurrection Anointing can flow outward to restore and revitalize this hurting world. God hasn't changed His modus operandi; Prayer, Praise and Worship is an irresistible combination which brings down the Glory Cloud of God upon His worshippers.

Having a willing, submitted and sold out temple to offer Him provides a reservoir for the Anointing to accumulate, then rush forth to heal the infirmities, feed the hungry and provide housing for the homeless.

Yes, the Holy Spirit also wants to provide material needs---but He's not our "Sugar Daddy!" He's not limited to Salvation, healings, stadium conferences or crusades; the Holy Spirit wants to break through into the Physical Realm and make this dump a descent and safe place to live!

The Lord accepted Solomon's prayer and appeared to him. The Lord gave Solomon the secrets of His eternal heart: If we would humble ourselves, confess our sins and inability to change ourselves, pray and seek His face, then He will bless, enable us to acquire health, wealth and prosperity of the soul; when our soul prospers, the rest of us will follow:

> "Beloved, I wish above all things that you may prosper and be in health, even as your soul prospers" (3 John 1:2). For the truth is: "A man can receive nothing, except it be given him from heaven" (John 3:27).

In the New Covenant and Dispensation of Grace, God no longer dwells in buildings made with human hands; our bodies are the vehicles to transport the Holy Spirit to communicate with humanity. We're temples of the living God (2 Corinthians 6:16).

God wants us to seek His face, turn from our wicked ways, live a blessed life by worshipping Him. He'll supply all our needs; what good father would withhold food, shelter, love, peace or wealth from his children whom he loves? Certainly, God the ultimate example of fatherhood is holy and righteous far above any human father, and will deliver what's needed.

We're ushered into God's Presence by the Holy Spirit. Through the blood of Jesus Christ, the Holy Spirit validates our right to boldly approach the throne of God.

So Praise and Worship amplifies our Faith; Faith gravitates the Holy Spirit to us. Then He transports our conscious presence to the Presence of the Divine.

God is our Creator and Father. He desires fellowship; in fact, He receives great pleasure out of fellowshipping with His spiritual offspring. He longs to hear our voice and to touch our spirit with His Spirit; then He can impart wisdom, understanding thereby developing an intimate, personal relationship with us. He wants to be our Father--the best Father we ever had! That's why He woos us close to Him and makes Covenants, Blessings and Promises.

To the contrary, it's not actually our trained singing voice that soothes God, but our attitude of Praise is a joyful noise to Him. When we offer Him Praise and Worship we offer Him Faith: It's Faith that pleases Him. Often, we don't sing aloud because we don't have an entertaining voice; yet God doesn't need to be entertained but worshipped. If we're singing praises for the entertainment or approval of the congregation, we might as well sit down.

As Christians we must remember to Pray, Praise and Worship Jesus with our children. We also should study the Word of God with them, meditate on His promises, and speak gracious words concerning Him, declaring our deliverance from trials and vices in our life; speak and testify to our answered prayers. We can invite our children into our devotions so they will know the Lord and appreciate Him as the One who brought us from darkness into His marvelous Light; then our children will anchor their Faith, Hope and dreams in Christ.

We don't want our children to be snared by the Devil, nor make the same mistakes and suffer the consequences of sin and disobedience as we did. Our rebellion and stubbornness caused us heartaches.

The Lord is our Good Shepherd. He has prepared for us a good life; this good life flourishes even in the wilderness of this sinful realm. Our Praise isn't just flattery with our lips, but fruit of our spirit having been prompted by the Holy Spirit.

We bless the Name of the Lord who is full of compassion; He forgives our sins, overlooks our faults and ministers to our needs. The Lord knows we're but dust with Life breathed into it; yet He has Mercy upon us for His Name's sake.

We come to God as humble as we know how, asking Him to forgive us for the many ways we sin and miss the mark. We worship at His feet and seek His Presence, the Kingdom and its righteousness, petitioning to be touched by His hand and receive the Anointing, the multitudes of His tender mercies and forbearances, thanking Him for the privilege to be called by His Name as His children.

We request that He lead us into the paths He had prepared for us to walk in before the foundation of the world. We worship His Name, knowing that Christ is the source of divine wisdom and comprehensive insight into the deep Mystery of the Triune Godhead.

When we receive visions and revelations we rejoice with unspeakkable joy and give Glory and honor to Christ the King. We stand behind the shield of His protection and sing Hallelujah, Glory!

We meet God intimately and bless His holy Name with our entire being. We remember His Word, Covenant, Promises and all the benefits of being Saved. He heals all our diseases and strengthens us with His mighty Presence. As we draw nearer to Him, His Anointing rubs off on us, so we can give it as a love offering to someone else.

When we meet the Christ within, He provides all our needs according to His riches in Glory. He's the righteous Judge; when oppressed we can always go to Him for relief. When we've sinned He quietly pulls us aside and tells us where we've missed the mark.

His mercies and judgments are from everlasting to everlasting, because He's the Alpha and Omega. We're blessed by keeping His Covenant: Faithfulness is the price we pay for the Blessing.

We meet Christ intimately within our spirit. As a minister of His Kingdom we meet Him daily in the inner conference room to discuss the present and future assignments in His world-wide ministry. We give thanks to Him for seeking to Save the lost.

We praise Him for He is our Savior and His reputation goes before Him. Every day we lift up His blessed Name for His greatness and unsearchable wisdom behind His mighty acts. We meditate on His majesty and goodness, and sing unto His righteousness.

His legacy, the memory of His faithfulness and love has been talked and written about for generations. He's Gracious, slow to anger, full of Compassion and capable of great Kindness. He's Good to all especially to those who Praise Him.

We are His saints, redeemed from the curse of the Law and Satan's manipulations of those Laws; we're rescued from a fate of eternal damnation and destruction. God heard our cry and pitied every groan; He delivered us from our captor.

Jesus Christ invites us to sit at the table with Him in His everlasting Kingdom. We who Pray, Praise and Worship Him make His coming back to the Physical Realm a lot sooner; Praise brings Him from His throne to fulfill the desires of our hearts. The Lord preserves those who love Him. O, if we would Praise the Lord!

God is Spirit

23 "...the true worshiper shall worship the Father in Spirit and in truth: For the Father seeks such to worship Him. 24 God is Spirit; and they that worship Him must worship Him in Spirit and in truth." John 4:23,24 (NKJV).

Jesus went down to Jacob's Well in Samaria. There He met a woman and asked her for a drink of water. The woman was surprised to see Jesus, a Jew down in that region; Samaria held a stigma--like the Ghetto Projects in a major city---Samaria was a region that no righteous Jew would be at unless he was up to no good.

According to the Jewish tradition, the Samaritans were half-breeds, dogs, and unclean as swine. Yet, Jesus loved them; the Son of Man trudged down to Samaria.

There were other wells which Jesus could've drank water from--but that woman wasn't at those wells. Neither did Jesus go down there to call this woman's sins to remembrance--there were plenty of sinners in Jerusalem and the surrounding areas. He arrived to give her the Living Water, the Word, His Resurrection Anointing to release ministry into her life.

Yes, she was a sinner--but so was everyone else. Jesus, being the Sinless One, arrived to share His righteousness with an outcast. She, not being Jewish had no Covenant with God that she knew of(The Gentiles didn't know that even a non-Jew if by Faith believed in God, the Covenants with Abraham and Moses would apply to them too; Ruth was a Moabite, a Gentile, and Jesus of Nazareth was born through this line of genealogy.).

But Jesus, Jehovah, the Covenant Maker stood before her and offered her the Living Water that would bring her into a Covenant relationship with Him, and satisfy her spiritual thirst forever; "...whosoever drinks of the water that I shall give him shall NEVER thirst; but the water that I shall give him shall be IN HIM A WELL OF WATER SPRINGING UP INTO EVERLASTING LIFE" (v.14).

When she asked for this Living Water, immediately the conversation advanced to the purpose Jesus came into her life: Worship --if the Samaritans held their peace and didn't Worship Him the rocks in Samaria would cry out!

The Father who knows the hearts of everyone, knew there was a veil, a curtain of prejudice that needed torn from top to bottom; there was also a common misconception concerning righteousness,---the who, what, when, where, how and the why in Worshipping God the Father.

Jesus confided in her; He told her He was the Messiah, Christ, the Anointed One; and the fullness of the time had come for the Samaritans, the outcasts, to know that God required Worship from everyone; that He will be gracious unto them at the hearing of their Prayers, Praise and Worship.

Everyone and everything in the Physical Realm that has breath must Praise the Lord, magnify and give thanks--Worship from the Human temple--not a mountain, building or city. Because God is Spirit and Man is also a spirit created in His image and likeness (after God's Spirit).

Anyone who worships God must Worship Him with their spirit by the prompting of the Holy Spirit; for the Father is looking for people willing to present themselves as a Living Sacrifice, Holy, which is our Reasonable Service.

As Born Again Christians, we often forget that we're spirit beings and capable of communicating with the Father of spirits --God.

Within our Human Spirit is the Holy Spirit, and the Holy Spirit is God. God communicates with us by His Presence within our recreated Human spirit; then the information or blessings are transmitted to our soul which houses the mind; now we can comprehend, understand or receive healing virtue.

We look up in the sky and pray to God, but the truth is that God also dwells in our spirit. He's not in an inaccessible, archangel-guarded place, but inside our spirit, which is surrounded by our sometimes rebellious temple of flesh. It's a mind boggling Mystery why God even dwells in such fragile containers.

After Salvation we must learn to Practice the Presence. This is done through applying our Faith in the Word of God. He's always with and in us; so we consciously acknowledge His Presence in our daily devotion and throughout the day; we speak to Him; we pray silently and aloud; and Worship, sing songs of Praise and lift Him up: Then He will come forth in Presence and power to the extent that even our natural senses will detect him.

When we Pray or Worship the Lord with our spirit, it's really the Holy

Spirit prompting the action. God uses our lips to Pray, Praise and Worship Himself! (in cooperation with our free will) It's also God who speaks healings, blessings and favor into the Physical Realm. This shouldn't surprise us, since He indwells us to advance His kingdom on Earth.

When we were unsaved we had no inclination or desire to Praise the Lord; now that we're Saved, why do we desire it now? It's the Presence and promptings of the Holy Spirit in Covenant with our soul and mind submitted to His voice; and the Holy Spirit says through our lips, "Praise the Lord!"

Here's another true Mystery: God assist us in what to pray for and how to pray, then answers Himself by granting the petition. This may sound like nonsense, but it's true!

Remember, it's the Holy Spirit who helps us to pray; how can we not get what we need if the Holy Spirit--who is God--is doing the praying and is the Provider? Will He prompt us to pray and not deliver? Will God turn down His own requests? Nay--He doesn't play games, neither will He withhold any good thing from us!

"For as many as are led by the Spirit of God, they are the sons of God. The Spirit bears record with our spirit, that we are the children of God" (Romans 8:14,16). It's the Holy Spirit who verifies that we're the Children of God. He also helps us to be God's Children, and testifies in our Human spirit by revelation that Jesus Christ is the Lord, and we should listen to His Word.

The Holy Spirit gives us boldness to witness the Word of God and to testify of His Goodness and Mercy in answering prayers.

In the early church, the disciples were forbidden to speak in the Name of Jesus. The disciples assembled together and lifted up their voices to God in one accord, and said:

"And now, Lord, behold their threats; and grant unto your servants, that with all boldness they may speak Your Word. By stretching forth Your hand to heal; and that signs and wonders may be done by the Name of Your holy child Jesus.

And when they had prayed, the PLACE WAS SHAKEN where they assembled together, and THEY WERE ALL FILLED WITH THE HOLY GHOST, and they spoke the Word of God with boldness" (Acts 4:18-31).

The Holy Spirit (called the Holy Ghost to designate He's a Person) changes people and circumstances. Prayer is sanctioned communication with God; and the Holy Spirit is God's Spirit; without the Holy Spirit God wouldn't be God---or wouldn't exist and be powerless.

This is the Holy Spirit we know and love:

> "Who, is clothed with honor and majesty; Who covers Himself with a garment of Light, and stretches out the heavens like a curtain; Who laid the beams of His chambers in the waters; Who makes the clouds His chariot, and walks upon the wings of the wind; Who makes angelic spirits and His ministers a flaming fire; Who laid the foundations of the earth, that it should not be moved forever" (Psalms 104:1-5).

Again the power of God manifested in response to an Italian centurion named Cornelius. He was "A devote man, and one that feared God with all his house, which gave much alms to the people (sowed seed into the Kingdom of God), and prayed to God always."

And the Lord said to him, "Your prayers and your alms are come up for a memorial before God" (V.1,2,4). Marvelous! His prayers and charity to the poor was remembered and became the object of MEMORIAL before God. It was something God couldn't ignore.

Cornelius had been pressing into the Kingdom for a long time. He couldn't touch the heart of God because he wasn't a Jew from one of the Twelve Tribes of Israel; as far as he knew, he wasn't included in the Old Testament Covenants of Promise.

But Jesus Christ died on the cross for Cornelius and Gentiles like him; By this act of Grace, the indwelling Holy Spirit opened the doors of Heaven for him, ushering him into the throne room of God; now he had a personal relationship with God.

For it was predestined that the Blessing of Abraham would come upon the Gentiles through Jesus Christ. The Lord told Cornelius to send for the Apostle Peter, who would lead him to the Throne of Grace.

Simon Peter was no different than other Jews in regard to the Gentiles. He was prejudice and ignorant of God's "grafting in" plan concerning the Gentiles, becoming joint-heirs in the Promise.

The Holy Spirit spoke to him in a vision, then audibly, as he was on the roof in meditation. The main focus of the vision was revelation knowledge: God is no respecter of persons. He told Peter, "Behold, three men seek you. Arise therefore, and get yourself down, and go with them, doubting nothing: for I have sent them" (v.19,20).

When Peter arrived, Cornelius fell down at Peter's feet and worshipped him. Peter panicked. He picked Cornelius up and told him that an Apostle is man--but the Lord Jesus Christ is the Messiah, worthy to be praised!

It was against Jewish ordinances for Peter to be in Cornelius' house; obedience to the Holy Spirit is better than sacrifices and traditions. Both men were fasting and praying at their homes when the Holy Spirit contacted them. Neither man knew they were in one accord with the plan of God. The Spirit of God walks throughout the earth searching for souls to Worship the Lord.

After Peter preached the Word of Life, the Anointing fell upon the Gentiles. They were Saved and Baptized in the Holy Spirit with the scriptural evidence of speaking in tongues.

Now the Cornelius Family could worship the Father in Spirit and in truth, because they possessed the Baptism in the Holy Spirit to usher them before the Presence of God.

> "For one who speaks in an [unknown] tongue speaks not to men but to God, for no one understands or catches his meaning, because in the [Holy] Spirit he utters secret truths and hidden things [not obvious to the understanding]. He that speaks in a [strange] tongue edifies and improves himself..." (1 Corinthians 14:2,4 Amp. Bible).

Many times we cannot perceive the Presence of Christ in our life because we expect to "feel" something with our external and mental senses. Often our attention, therefore our heart and treasure is in the world and the pleasures of participating in it.

Fasting and prayer is the key to getting back on track; it's a sacrifice and offering to God; it humbles the soul (mind, will and emotions) and weakens the strength of the physical body by denying it pleasures; it therefore crucifies it. By this the regenerated Human spirit encasing the Holy Spirit is exalted which brings us before the Presence. Faith is a Bridge which transports us from where we are in the natural to where

Christ sits upon the throne.

The situations and temptations of life can become a sweat-less victory if we would Worship in the Spirit and let the Master Builder of creation solve our problems.

By divine right God rules creation; only with our permission can He be both Savior and Lord of our life. Praying in the Spirit is Christ expressing Himself in and through us to manifest His plans, purposes, and pursuits.

As much as we want our children to take baths, even more does God wants His children to take baths---in the Holy Spirit and speak with tongues; and manifest His Anointing. This Anointing is on His shed Blood; it's also on the Word and Name of Jesus: Jesus is God's righteousness revealed.

We must know Him and the power out-flowing from His Resurrection. Through obedience, faithfulness to the promptings of the Holy Spirit, the supernatural Christ can solve our personal and social problems.

The Holy Spirit desires to minister in the areas of drugs, violence, lawlessness in schools and streets, national and international crisis, sickness, hunger and poverty. The Spirit is compassionate concerning the plight of twentieth century Man: The plagues of AIDS, Ebola, Leprosy, Cancer, Criminality, Insanity, Suicide, Crack, and depression. He wants to help us rise up against the demonic spirits who are bent on murdering us.

The Holy Spirit is fire; He's always fired up. We're the ones who become lukewarm, cold, and say, The Devil doesn't bother me. If we leave the Devil alone--don't even mention his name--he'll leave us alone. But the Devil is a murderer; he's aggressive, an oppressor, relentless, the master deceiver.

If Satan's not coming against us it's because he already has us: We need to check our relationship with Christ. If there are no "difficulties" in life: When was the last time we witnessed for Christ, studied the Word or prayed? When was the last time we attended church or Prayer Meeting? Are our tithes up to date? Is there someone we know in the hospital or jail that we haven't visited?

If the Devil isn't bothering us we could be backslidden in some area. Satan is the sworn enemy of God and His family. Satan has already stolen our terrestrial inheritance; we're only taking back from him what already belongs to us, thus enforcing the victory won by Jesus Christ at Calvary.

Even in the natural, when military forces take important ground, they just can't leave and expect it to remain in their hands; they must occupy the area taken and enforce their victory; even so, when a builder clears land from the wilderness and builds a house, he can't just walk away, because the wilderness will reclaim the land; even so must Christians occupy and remain vigilant less the Devil will come back and take what's been won for us by Jesus at Calvary. He can't take it from Jesus, because all this was given to us, and it's our responsibility to hold onto it.

Many Saints live quiet, complacent yet defeated lives; they appease the Devil. But we're radical people: Complacency comes at the expense of missing God, by not rendering to Him Praise and Worship. Praise and Worship is Spiritual Warfare!

Praise and Worship makes the Devil angry. If he comes against us we have authority to rebuke him in the Name of Jesus Christ. We must never cease to praise Jesus and bring down the Glory Cloud so thick that it chokes the Devil! He'll run away depressed by his spirit of depression.

It's not our inheritance to live a defeated, miserable life; that's not victory in Jesus. We may sing victory songs but true victory arrives when a spirit of Prayer, Praise and Worship rises up in us, inspiring Faith and obedience to Christ. This brings soundness of spirit, soul and body, the wealthy place that God predestined before the foundation of the world.

Victory in Jesus is amazing Grace. His Grace manifests in His faithfulness to all generations. His will is for us to spiritually and materially prosper even as our children's children prospers.

God is a good God, and the Devil is a bad Devil; it's not difficult to figure out who's doing what to us!

If we believe that its God's will for us to be oppressed by sickness and poverty, then why do we go to the hospital to get well? Wouldn't we be disobeying God? And why do we accept secular promotions, raises, invest in company 401K Plans, stocks, bonds or real estate properties, if we believe it's God's will to be poor? Does He gets pleasure or Glory from our poverty? No! People who say "it's God's" will for things that are Satan's doings are usually the first at the Casinos or Lottery Line--- trying to get "blessed" with finances they didn't work for!

Also, giving to God's cause is worship. If we have nothing to give on a material level, how can we help those in need. God gives us the ability to get wealth so we can Praise Him for and with it.

Many of us have become too unreasonable--even un-teachable--and miss the Person of Jesus Christ and His inheritance. Remember, He incarnated into the Physical Realm to raise up the name of the dead, our name, upon our Inheritance. The least we can do is Praise and Worship Him: Seek the Giver not the gift.

> 25 "And at midnight Paul and Silas prayed, and sang praises unto God; and the prisoners heard them. 26 And suddenly there was a great earthquake, so that the foundations of the prison were shaken: and immediately all the doors were opened, and everyone's bands were loosed" Acts 16:25-26 (KJV).

As Paul and Silas traveled to spread the Gospel, they encountered a slave girl who had an unclean spirit using her to speak into the Physical Realm; it was a spirit of divination. She introduced the Apostles and their purpose for being in that city. But Paul wanted to socialize with the people and get to know them before preaching to them.

The Lord doesn't employ demonic spirits to prepare the way for Him; In the Gospels, Jesus rebuked the unclean spirit who announced that He was the Christ.

The Apostle Paul, being grieved of her untimely and demonic presence, rebuked and cast out the evil spirit resident inside her. Perhaps Paul thought he was also doing her a favor. But her master lost his edge in business negotiations; she foretold the future for him.

Immediately, the Demonic Kingdom focused their influence on these two Apostles. The people rioted, claiming the apostles taught customs that were unlawful for Romans to observe. The magistrates ripped the Apostle's clothes off, beat them and threw them in prison. It didn't look promising.

Under these circumstances, today's Christians would be infuriated, calling Channel 4, the top Law Firm and threatening lawsuits.

In Silas' place, we might say to Paul, "Look what you got me into! I'm bleeding to death and my reputation is ruined! It was your idea to preach to these crazy Gentiles! Paul--you missed it--the Holy Spirit couldn't have told you to come here!"

Throbbing pain would've caused many of us to lay there, conserve our strength and think up some legal maneuver or plea bargain to get out of jail, and the death sentence that would follow in the Morning.

But Paul and Silas prayed and sang praises unto God; and the prisoners heard them. Yes, the Apostles weren't humming or moaning Zion songs but actually SINGING and rejoicing from their hearts. Even the prisoners, who had most likely been beaten too, cursed and complained, thought the Apostles were either drunk or the toughest men on earth.

Who in the world are these strangers, who when beaten sing glad songs? Who's the God they serve, who enables them to love their enemies? The Praise of the Apostles was their testimony that Jesus was alive in their hearts. Living Faith is what people notice, not just the memorization and quoting of the Holy Scriptures.

Their prayers and songs of Praise were like two candles in that dark dungeon; the food was terrible, the conditions were inhuman, and the treatment was harsh--but in that corner of the dungeon Hope emerged--Living Water flowed into the hearts of the prisoners and chased away the evil. They brought the Holy Fire.

The prison was shaken, the doors creaked open, the shackles on everyone's feet snapped off, the yokes upon their souls were destroyed and the captives set free.

Yet no one escaped from the dungeon. This made the jailer grateful, otherwise he would have killed himself, as not to give the Romans the pleasure. But the Gospel was preached; the jailer and his household got Saved.

We should be the type of Christians it can be said: "These that have turned the world upside down are come here also" (Acts 17:6). Truly our Prayers, Praises and Worship can turn the world upside down if we will offer them. For out of our belly shall flow rivers of Living Waters--rivers of miracles from Him who lives forever: Glory to the Lamb of God!

Via Della Rosa, The Way of Suffering is also the life of Jesus of Nazareth. To know Him is to know of His suffering; it's to weep over the "Jerusalem" in every country; to groan and be troubled in our spirit when we encounter sickness, hunger, poverty, or inhumanity. If we contemplate upon His and our death upon the cross will bring fresh revelations. There are countless levels to knowing Christ; suffering with persecution for His cause is something we should be prepared to do; suffering is our also reasonable service.

Yet some Christians want the benefits without the cost or labor. We don't want to pay the price. We want the personal relationship and the Anointing but not the "fellowship of His suffering" that comes with it.

Do we really want the personal, supernatural, intimate, progressive relationship that Paul wrote about in Phil. 3:10-12., or only the historical Jesus written about in the Bible? Is He the Unknown God?

The Spirit of God flared inside the Apostle Paul and led him to the City of Athens, Greece. On arrival Paul found the city OVERTHROWN BY SPIRITS OF IDOLATRY; there was no better place for Paul to be; for the Holy Spirit used him mightily.

Immediately, the philosophers and theologians brought Paul to the Aeropagus to hear his doctrine. The Grecians spent a lot of time studying and debating old and new doctrines; they thought the more they knew the better they were.

The Holy Spirit prompted Paul to take notice of an inscription on an altar: TO THE UNKNOWN GOD. Paul reasoned that this inscription was an attempt by the religious leaders to know the Person of God: The Unknown God was honored just in case in the worship of the other gods, he would be excluded.

The Unknown God was not the God of Israel; it was only one of several false gods. Nevertheless, Paul capitalized on the superstition of the Grecians to tell them about Jesus of Nazareth and Him being raised from the dead.

The Grecians were amazed; they entertained the possibility of the resurrection of the dead and thought Paul worth hearing: How could a man named Jesus of Nazareth find favor with God and be raised from the dead?

The philosophers were accustomed to talking about gods made out of natural materials; they had eyes but couldn't see; mouths they had but couldn't speak; hands had they but couldn't save; they also had legs and feet but couldn't walk--Certainly, Paul's God was intriguing!

Moses told Israel, Take heed: "And before you lift up your eyes unto heaven, and when you see the sun, and the moon, and the stars, even all the host of heaven, should be driven [by Satan] to worship them, and serve them... Take heed unto yourselves, before you forget the Covenant of the LORD your God, which He made with you, and make you a graven image, or the likeness of anything, which the LORD your God has forbidden you" (Deu.4:19,23).

Some of them likely said to one another, "Moses, you must think we're stupid. Why would we do such a wicked thing? But they wound up doing jus that---worshipping golden calves and idols!

Are we worshipping the Unknown God like the Grecians? Do we KNOW Jesus Christ as our Savior and Lord? Is it possible, highly probable, we've missed Him and found dry religion instead? These are serious questions we must honestly ask ourselves. The evidence that we're Saved is the Presence of Christ in us. His Presence manifests in us as a changed life.

Whereas, before we embraced sin, but now we loathe to sin. Before we praised ourselves and our material possessions--our plastic Visa god--but now we've exchanged these things for the Living God. Before we cursed God and served the host of the lower heavens: Satan's cults, psychics, tarot readers, palm readers, celebrities, sciences and religions; but ran from Jesus, the lover of our soul.

Now we proclaim: What a Word is this!

There has to be a behavioral change: The wicked things we used to do we don't do anymore; the bars and parties we used to haunt we don't haunt anymore.

Before we may have gone to church but our bible collected dust all week--that has also changed, because the Lord has made a great change in our life. Now we look forward to going to church, Prayer Meetings and Bible Studies. Our selfish agenda has gone out the window; we were blind now we can see.

We eagerly serve His Plans, Purposes and Pursuits. Through our faithfulness, we have become useful vessels fit for the Master's use. Having been filled unto overflowing capacity with His Spirit, we no longer are the Human host for every unclean and hateful spirit. We aren't slaves to sin.

The Lord Jesus Christ is unknown to a lot of people. The Love of

Christ constrains us to win the lost at any cost. We can Worship the Lord by winning souls into His Kingdom. The one who wins souls is wise; and Christ is the Wisdom and Power of God. Winning souls manifests the Presence, Person and Anointing of Christ.

Witnessing is a form of Worship. Paul went to Greece: Maybe we will never witness overseas, but we can finance those who will. We can finance missionary journeys similar to the ones Paul went on. Our unselfish sowing into the Kingdom brings us closer to knowing the Giver of all Life. "Let him who glories glory in this, that he understands and knows Me, that I AM the LORD" (Jeremiah 9:24).

THE RESURRECTION COVENANTS

17 "...it was dark, behold a smoking furnace, and a burning lamp that passed between those pieces. 18 In the same day the LORD made Covenant with Abraham." Gen. 15:17,18 (KJV)

This wasn't a backyard family barbecue thrown in Abraham's honor. This ceremony was historical. It ratified the Abrahamic Covenant, and focused on a personal relationship between Abraham, his descendents and Christ. Through the Abrahamic Covenant, Man was justified by his Faith in the Word and Name (reputation) of God; Faith in God was now counted as righteousness (right standing with God).

The blood was the medium by which sin was remitted and Covenants, God-to-Man agreements were established. The life of the blood was applied to the Covenant and that made it a valid seal, "...for the blood is the life" (Deuteronomy 12:23).

God walked in the pooled blood between the sacrificed animals. He imparted in the blood the terms and provisions of the Covenant. The Abrahamic Covenant became the Legal Document that God could channel His exceedingly great power into the Physical Realm, thereby super-natural miracles, signs and wonders could be performed by anyone exercising genuine Faith.

Though God is Omniscient, Omnipresent and Omnipotent when God makes Covenant or Promises He limits Himself from doing the opposite or something different to keep His Word.

Obviously, God can enter the Physical Realm whenever He pleases

Yet, neither God or Satan have a "legal right" to live here or operate independently of Humans in this material realm.

This is because God gave the Title Deed of Authority and Dominion of the Physical Realm to Adam (In the Garden of Eden). Therefore, Man is the legal owner of the Physical Universe; it's equally true that God or Satan can operate, exercise their wills in this world through Human Beings; and that's what they do.

God and Satan are spirit beings. Man is a spirit too; but Man has been given a physical body, an "earth suit." Thus Man is Hu (dirt) and Man (spirit); a spirit in a dirt body. Therefore, Man is the only legal spirit, true resident entitled to live and procreate, in his image and likeness, in the Physical Realm (not counting animals who don't have spirits etc...).

Since Man is the legal resident in this realm, he can cast out devils, because devils have no legal right to inhabit Human Beings---unless invited in through sinful behaviors and agreements directly related to the operations of the powers of darkness. Even the Holy Spirit MUST have our permission before He can indwell us.

Therefore, when God created the Physical Realm, He Covenanted with Adam (Man); when God Covenanted with Man, He limited Himself and became subject to His own Covenant Word. And since God won't break His Word, He continues to cooperate with Man, indwell Man, and channels His power through Man. With Man, God has His will done on earth as it is in Heaven.

The same way we became legal residents (being born here), the dirt body of Jesus of Nazareth made Christ, the Word a legal resident in the physical arena.

Being the Creator of the Physical Realm wouldn't fulfill the legal requirements for residency. God needed a person to agree with Him, a person who was already a legal resident of the Earth. Then He could reveal His Person and creative powers. Abraham, the Old Testament prophets and Jesus of Nazareth received the same Holy Spirit and ministered Blessings and the Promises by the Spirit.

It was Christ who spoke out of heaven and swore by Himself the immutability of the Oath Blessing, the divine endowment, empowerment and guarantee that God wouldn't renege or fail to keep His Word (Genesis 22:16). Like Abraham, Jesus depended on the unchanging nature of the Father's Covenant Word.

Being convinced and knowing beyond a shadow of doubt that God cannot lie, we believe that He's no respecter of persons. The provisions in the Covenant reflect the image of His Person and the source of His endless Life upon those who accept and enter the Covenant.

Neither Human, angel or demon can intimately know Christ outside of His Covenant; but only Human beings can know Him as both Savior and Lord. Heavenly angelic spirits may Worship and Praise Him, but cannot intimately know Christ personally as Savior and Lord.

Hence, to know Christ is to be a partner in His Covenant, even a partaker of His eternal attributes and inheritance. From this point of view: "Even when we were dead in sins, has quickened us together with Christ ...And has raised us up together, and made us sit together in heavenly places in Christ Jesus" (Ephesians 1:5,6).

From where we sit with Him in Heaven we perceive Who He is and who we are in relation to Him; all He accomplished at Calvary becomes real to us. We also discover the reliability of the Word, Name, and Blood; they're inseparable from the Person of Christ, and the power out-flowing from His Resurrection.

God's Rhema (Word) goes forth like a mighty river flowing from His Throne downward into the Physical Realm. When the Word encounters us He impresses upon our consciousness the will of the Father. If we, like Jesus answer His promptings with obedience and Faith then all is well; but if we respond to the Word negatively, there's no Life imparted and we remain in darkness.

"In the beginning was the Word", was what the Apostle John wrote; and the Word is God. So that's why the Word is so important in Covenant: The Word is Christ, God's impartation of His Person, image and Life.

The Word is precious (1 Samuel 3:1). Without the Word of God, there's no vision and the people perish (Proverbs 29:18). The same Word is our Rock; the Word is settled in Heaven. We must also let it be settled in our heart. It's our duty as Christians to settle the Word on the Earth in our family, community, nation and the entire world.

The Rhema is all that God is; God won't be or do anything apart from His Word. We cannot accept Him without His Word and vice versa. His Word hidden in our hearts keeps us from habitually sinning. The Word is a light to guide our feet and light our pathway.

God's Name (reputation) is great and above all other names; but He has magnified His Word above His Name (Psalms 138:2). God's Name is Holy; but His Word is His immutable Oath.

If His Word should fail, and therefore become unreliable, then His Name would suffer loss. If God would break His Covenant, He would have to redefine His Holiness, Righteousness and Truth. Everything proceeded and proceeding out of Him would be affected.

"The heavens declare the glory of God; and the firmament show His handiwork" (Psalms 19:1). All creation is to the Praise of His Glory, that everything that has breath Praise Him: Why, because He's holy!

If God would tell one lie EVERYTHING would immediately change; the repercussion would be like a million imploded suns gone super nova at once, whose energy and shock wave would span eternity; even God's future Plans, Purposes and Pursuits in creation would change.

He would have to vindicate Lucifer, now called Satan, and give him back his original position and authority as the Guardian Cherub; God would have to restore every fallen angel that rebelled with Lucifer; God would be forced to admit every living and departed sinner from Earth and Hell into heaven; and He would apologize to the sodomites and homosexuals of Sodom and Gomorrah for killing them!

God could no longer punish sin if He became a liar. When Man broke one of the Ten Commandments, he broke them all: If God breaks one of His commandments He has also broken them all; and this just cannot happen.

There is no forgiveness of sin for God; like there was no Redemption Plan for the rebellious Lucifer and angels that sinned--they were cast to the lower realms. So how can God judge us or anyone else if He lost His Righteousness, His ability to Judge, even Justify (declare Not Guilty)the Guilty through Faith in Jesus Christ?

"My Covenant will I not break, nor alter the thing that is gone out of My lips" (Psalms 89:34). His Word becomes His limitation, yet God will NEVER go back on His Word. He sets limits, perimeters on Himself--slows Himself down so we can understand and work as partners with Him through Covenant.

But we suffer when we fail to keep our end of the agreement: HIS SELF-IMPOSED LIMITATIONS ALSO PREVENTS HIM FROM DOING OUR PART OF THE COVENANT, causing us to live in the shadows instead of the sunshine.

> "For the Word of God is quick and powerful, and sharper than any two-edged sword, piercing even to the dividing asunder of soul and spirit, and of the joints and marrow, and is a discerner of the thoughts and intents of the heart" (Hebrews 4:12).

It's a mystery why God loves us. The Word of God knows the thoughts and intents of our heart (which are often wicked) and He still loves us. Nothing is hidden from the two-edged sword of the Spirit. Because the Word is alive--not just a collection of the thoughts of God--the Word can change us.

The sword of the Word can instantly separate the thoughts of the Human spirit from the thoughts of the mind. We need to know when it's the Holy Spirit leading us or our own mind misleading us. The Word divides and separates the holy life from the profane worldly life, and Righteousness from unrighteousness in the decision making process of our life. Meditating on the Word will expose the truth of God and release His Resurrection Anointing, the restoration and reconciliation power into any situation.

The Word seeks us as we seek Him; Like water seeks its level so the Word seeks His level of expression in us. While we're scanning Heaven with our spiritual senses and looking for someplace to land, the Word of God leads and guides us as runway lights mark the lane for our safe landing.

He wants us to find Him more than we do, and the fellowship of Jesus Christ. When we sound the depths of the Word, we discover that Christ is our exceedingly great reward. If we seek the Word, the Person of Christ--not only will we have the Giver but the gifts too. There's Life in the Word. Let not the Word of Life depart from before our eyes!

> 2 "And God spoke unto Moses, and said unto him, I AM the LORD: 3 And I appeared unto Abraham, unto Isaac, and unto Jacob, by the Name of God Almighty (El Shaddai), but My Name JEHOVAH was I not known to them. 4 And I have also established My Covenant with them, to give them the land..."

Exodus 6:2-4 (KJV)

Jehovah is the Name of God who makes and keeps Covenants. The Godhead is Triune; there are three distinct manifestations of God and each has an unique purpose in creation. This truth makes it more difficult for us to comprehend the depths of His Person--there being three-in-one.

Yet God expresses Himself as a Covenant-making and promise-keeping Jehovah (Jesus). He does this to establish a trustworthy Name for Himself, a solid eternal reputation, making it possible and truthful for the Apostle Paul to declare: "Neither is there Salvation in any other: For there is none other Name under Heaven given among men, whereby we must be Saved" (Acts 4:12).

Jehovah proclaims there is no other God besides Him in Heaven or on Earth. Though people may know God by other names describing His attributes--He revealed Himself to Moses as JEHOVAH, the God who makes Covenants. His Covenant-making nature is only an attribute of His personality.

Jehovah encompasses the Name (Reputation) of Jesus Christ: "Wherefore God also hath highly exalted Him, and given Him a Name which is above every name: That at the Name of Jesus every knee should bow, of things in Heaven, and things in Earth, and things under the Earth; and that every tongue confess that Jesus Christ is Lord, to the Glory of God the Father" (Philippians 2:9-11).

The fellowship of the Spirit is through Jesus Christ. As the Word/Christ, He made Himself of no reputation and incarnated into the physical world.

After His Resurrection, He was conferred (given) by the Father the Name above all other names; the Name conferred upon the Man named Jesus of Nazareth crowned Him the "embodied" Savior and Lord; as Christ the Word dwelled within Jesus, so the vessel of Jesus was transformed into the image of Christ the Lord.

Mary was impregnated with the Word, the Father's spiritual Seed to form a body in the likeness of sinful flesh; the Blood flowing through the veins of Jesus wasn't the blood of Mary or a Human male: The Blood was "J" Type--Jehovah's Blood.

This was because the blood of Adam's descendents was impure, tainted; it transmitted Adamic Sin; therefore all Human Beings are born in sin. But, the Blood of God was an unique biological and Spirit-Life with redemptive properties. Jehovah's Blood (later called the Blood of Jesus) was exchanged for the release from sin and death of Adam and his descendents; it was the Atonement.

At Jesus' birth He became a legal resident of the Physical Realm. At the age of thirty, Jesus of Nazareth received the Baptism in the Holy Spirit and fire. He was one hundred percent Man and one hundred percent God. God's Name was established on the Earth.

The Mighty One is here!

> 8 "And Moses took the blood, and sprinkled it on the people, and said, Behold the Blood of the Covenant."

God made Covenant with Abraham and his descendants. This Covenant was based on Obedience and Faith. The Resurrection Anointing to create miracles, signs and wonders was the power resident in the Abrahamic Covenant. The prophets of Israel performed miracles through this Covenant, though they ministered to a people bound under the Mosaic Covenant of laws, rituals and ordinances; miracles were actuated by Genuine Faith, not ordinances.

Yet the house of Israel remained rebellious. They backslid and refused to walk by Faith, but instead worshipped the host of heaven, the false gods and traditions of their neighbors.

The Mosaic Law was instituted in response to Israel's inability or refusal to walk by Faith and not by sight. Israel's lust of the flesh, the eyes, and the pride of life disqualified them from walking with the Lord in the Abrahamic Covenant.

The Book of the Law was sprinkled with blood, then the congergation was sprinkled to bring them into agreement with the Mosaic Covenant.

The Law was like religion: Religion has no power, no Anointing to destroy yokes or the evil nature of Man. So the Law was only an instrument to *teach* the principles of Obedience, what Holiness means (through clean and unclean animals, objects and places etc), and about Sin. To the end they would also learn about having Genuine Faith in God and His Word.

Nevertheless, because the Law was given by God it necessitated that it be confirmed with blood. The inability of the Law to change the behavior of Human Beings, allowed Satan to administer guilt, condemnation and the fear (terror) of death.

The Law's divine purpose was to prepare the hearts of Israel for the upcoming dispensation of Grace; for Grace and Truth came by Jesus Christ. He's the Way, the Truth and the Life.

The Mosaic Law was a type of the real Hope, the Resurrection of the Dead. Those under the Law had the Hope of the Resurrection and not the Resurrection itself, not the Person who is the Resurrection and the Life.

The Law and religion talk about a future hope--but it's Faith— the naming and claiming the Resurrection and the Life, that gives us the victory.

For two thousand years, Christians celebrate with great enthusiasm the birth of Jesus of Nazareth (has become the great commercialization of Christmas). Truly, we're joyful that He arrived. Yet it was mainly His death and Resurrection that brought Eternal Life.

So let's not get too fuzzy about the cute and cuddly baby Jesus--He didn't know anymore about God or the world than we did at birth! It's Jesus the adult, the Lord, the Messiah, the Resurrected One we need to get acquainted with!

> 19 "And He took the bread, and gave thanks, and brake it, and gave unto them, saying, This is My body which is given for you; this do in remembrance of Me. 20 Likewise also the cup after supper, saying, This cup is the NEW TESTAMENT in My Blood, which is shed for you" Luke 22:19,20 (KJV)

The physical body of Jesus represented the veil of the temple. His body was the Door to the abode of the Father. His body was also the heavenly Ark of the Covenant, where God met the mortal High Priest who represented humanity at the Mercy Seat. Jesus represented the heavenly and the physical universe, He being both God and Man.

His body is symbolically eaten in remembrance of His sacrifice for sins. He told His followers, "Except ye eat the flesh of the Son of Man, and drink His blood, you have no life in you. Whosoever eats My flesh, and drinks My Blood, has Eternal Life; and I will raise him up at the last day" (John 7:53,54).

He also told them that He was the manna that came down from Heaven. Many people walked away because they were offended at His sayings. But Jesus was preparing them for the day His Blood would atone for their sins, and bring into reality the New Testament Covenant. He that partakes of His body and Blood partakes of the Covenant; and by the Covenant he shall live forever.

> "How much more shall the Blood of Christ, who through the Eternal Spirit offered Himself without spot to God" Heb. 9.14 (KJV)

While the first veil was standing, the way to the Most Holy Place wasn't open. But through the body of Jesus, the veil in the temple was torn from top to bottom.

Jesus was pierced and His blood ran down the cross; through His death on the cross the realm of Heaven was made available to Believers. As priests and kings of God, we can visit as citizens of both realms, and enjoy fellowship with our Father.

It wasn't through the Mosaic Covenant, the offering of animal sacrifices that appeased the Justice and Righteousness of God, but the Jehovah-Blood than flowed in the veins of Jesus of Nazareth; Who as High Priest entered with His own Blood into the Most Holy Place, and poured out His offering upon the Mercy Seat in the heavenly Sanctuary.

The Old Testament prophets declared, Thus says the LORD! But Jesus said, Verily, verily, I say unto you! God manifested Jehovah/Jesus for us. He'll do everything His Word says He'll do. His Word includes every scripture written in the Holy Bible. Seeing that He's faithful to His partners--us--we shouldn't have a problem Praying, Praising and Worshipping Him with our entire spirit, soul, body, and finances.

The Goodness of God leads us to Worship. His Goodness, Love and Kindness compels us to lift up His Name; and if we lift Him up from the earth, He'll draw everyone to Himself.

> "God is faithful, by whom you WERE CALLED UNTO THE FELLOWSHIP OF HIS SON JESUS CHRIST our Lord" (1 Corinthians 1:9). Yes, we're called to fellowship with Jesus Christ. It's not by accident that we seek and find Him. But now that we'

ve found Him, we must be especially careful how we treat Him. We form Human relationships through faithful communication and love; we also form our spiritual relationship with the Lord Jesus Christ the same way.

Notes

CHAPTER SIX
SERPENTS IN OUR GARDEN

It was God's perfect will that His image creation, Adam and his descendents be the "government" of the Physical Realm: "And God said unto them, Be fruitful, and multiply, and replenish the earth, and SUBDUE IT: and HAVE DOMINION..." (Genesis 1:26-28).

The above scripture has been sermonized and expounded on for thousands of years; the priests, scribes, prophets, theologians and latter day Christians agree that Adam was a far superior being than modern man.

Yet few consider the magnitude of these scriptures: From inhabitant too god requires deeper revelation--but in the scriptures are words such as "subdue" and "dominion" implying kingship or godhood.

In short, Adam was the god of the Physical Realm. When the angels asked the Lord, What is Man that He would fellowship and visit him in the Garden of Eden, the reply was: He made Man a little lower than the angels (in the original Hebrew Text, the term Elohim, meaning God, is used), and CROWNED HIM WITH GLORY AND HONOR, and put EVERYTHING under his feet (Psalms 8:3-9).

Then by default and transgression, Adam conceded the throne of the world to Lucifer; Adam forfeited the Title Deed to the Physical Realm. Now, instead of God potentially having nine planets and numerous moons populated with awesome spirit beings, giants in Faith governing futuristic cities--He has only the earth with smoggy cities, violence and crime, but a super Salvation plan to make Christians out of the spiritually dead.

Yet there remains the Mystery that had been hidden for ages: A wealthy place (Psalms 66:12) and heavenly dignity waiting to be appropriated, tapped into, by His children.

> 11 "For I know the thoughts and plans I have for you, says the LORD, thoughts and plans for WELFARE and PEACE and NOT FOR EVIL, to GIVE YOU HOPE IN YOUR FINAL OUTCOME" Jeremiah 29:11-13 (KJV).

The Lamb of God was slain before the foundation of the world. He was slain before Adam ever sinned. Therefore, the thoughts that God had concerning Man and the wealthy place and state of dignity was finished in the mind of God; it wasn't affected by what happened in the Garden of Eden; God works from the end backwards, thus "declaring the end from the beginning." And Satan cannot do that!

His salvation plan was the only provision that took into consideration Adam would fall. God is omniscient: He knew that Lucifer and Adam would fall. In Christ was manifested all the treasures of divine Wisdom and insight into the ways and purposes of God.

The Blessing: Endowment, the wealthy state of spiritual, mental, physical, and material prosperity--nothing missing, nothing broken-- was hidden in the Person of Christ, and revealed by the Holy Spirit.

Satan wants to possess our entire inheritance. But the truth of the matter is, much of it he cannot comprehend or appropriate for evil intent, nor can we access it for selfish motives.

The eternal Blessing is the habitation of Christ in us. The Blessing releases us from the yokes and bondages of life. God, who cannot lie, promised the Blessing before the world began, is our guarantee to an expected end. From the beginning, God envisioned us as being in Christ, when Satan saw us as sinners in his image and doing his dark bidding.

God is certain about His thoughts towards us. He's certain that He can bring to pass all that He envisions. He can and will bring us to the path He's foreordained for us to walk in--the expected end of this journey. When we pray He'll answer; as we seek Him with all our heart we shall find Him. He'll say, Well done My good and faithful servant!

God's kind intent was and still is to restore, resurrect and repurpose spiritual Israel and the church. He Made Covenant with Abraham to bless and be a blessing to his descendents. As the Covenant is an agreement that requires a response and participation from both parties, God was and remains faithful to His end of the agreement.

In the past and even today Israel struggles with the demonic powers of this world who are bent on stealing, killing and destroying whatever relationship Israel has with Jehovah: Now, the earthbound church is Satan's target.

The wealth of the wicked is stored up for the righteous: The wealth of the Old Testament Canaanites was stored up for Israel (Israel means Prince of God). The citizens of Canaan were only caretakers of the land, cities, livestock and material goods, because, "The earth is the LORD'S and the fullness thereof; the world, and they that dwell therein" (Psalms 24:1). But the Canaanites didn't know the Lord, that He created everything and could give it to whom He please; and because in the beginning he gave it to Adam (Man), He could choose which group in the Family of Man to occupy it.

God told Israel (meaning the Prince of God) as He tells us of the wealthy place, a large place (Psalms 18:19), and all we kings and priests have to do is POSSESS and press into the Blessing.

For Israel, the way was straight and narrow; the door was open and the Lord stood at the door to welcome them. All they had to do was stretch out their hands in Faith--grab hold of the unseen hand of God and possess the inheritance. Then they could enter into the rest and peace of the Lord.

> 30 "Let us go up at once, and possess it: For we are well able to overcome it. 31 But the men that went up with him said, we be not able to go up against the people: For they are stronger than we" Nu. 13:30,31 (KJV).

In the above Scriptures are some of the saddest verses in the Holy Bible. The fulfillment of a long awaited Promise was within hours of possession. But at the border---where breakthroughs occur---Satan snatched their meat and gave them a bone to chew on.

From Egypt to Canaan, the Israelites bickered, murmured and complained against Moses, yet made it to the border of the Promised Land. But behind the veil, unclean spirits stopped them cold in their tracks, and their hearts frosted over with the spirit of fear.

To the natural eye the land was what God said it was; God never told them the Promised Land was without obstacles; He didn't tell them the faithless could inherit the Promise; nor did He tell them to conquer Canaan in their own strength; but the Lord of the armies of Heaven would fight their battles.

They forming a committee; the twelve spies sent was more a council decision than a commandment of God. Moses sent the espionage team to investigate the territory and reveal to him the mililitary positions, troop strength and fortifications. Moses already believed God concerning the abundance of the wealthy place; the team report was designed to strengthen the Faith of the weak congregation.

The spies were supposed to report directly to Moses, who was the leader of Israel; Moses was God's delegated authority on Earth. Instead the men spoke directly to the congregation.

The spies gave plenty of positive reasons why to enter the Promised Land. They claimed the land was as God had said; most had doubted the accuracy of God's description. Ten of the spies negatively focused on the military portion of the investigation. They overemphasized the possible deaths and causalities if a war started, but downplayed God's Promise.

Talk of giants and walled cities caused a plague of demonic hysteria; fear broke out like a horrible rash amongst the congregation; but they didn't have the Faith to believe and realize that with God on their side, one Israelite could defeat twelve Canaanites!

Caleb silenced the congregation and took the righteous stand, "We are well able to overcome it." Caleb knew Jehovah, the Covenant God-- that He was more than able to keep His Promise. Caleb knew if Israel would trust in and rely on His Word, all things were possible to them that believe.

Unfortunately, the ten spies insisted, "We be not able to go up against the people for they are stronger than we." The congregation refused to believe the report of the Lord and His two servants.

Israel shrieked in terror at the thought of one drop of their precious blood being shed. The opinions based on natural facts and the faithlessness of the ten spies became "truth" to the congregation.

The gospel truth was what God said, but facts were what the spies saw with their natural eyes. Hence, Satan promoted as truth what their natural eyes saw; Satan and his servants succeeded in keeping the inheritance from Israel.

The demonic authorities used witchcraft to manipulate, intimidate and finally dominate Israel. They revisited Israel's slave mentality, struck at their inferiority complexes, phobias, rebellion and unbelief in their own God. Aided by the powers of the unclean spirits, the Canaanites became larger than life; fear became pay dirt as the forces of darkness overwhelmed the former slaves with the terror of giant fleshly monsters roaming the Promised Land looking to eat them and their children.

These spirits knew that Israel didn't know or even trust Jehovah their God; the unclean spirits knew God better than Israel. It wasn't difficult for them to scare the fight out of the children of Israel, and persuade them that victory was impossible and resistance was futile.

The demonic spirits occupying the Promised Land and ruling the territory from their unseen thrones, knew they were subject to God's Word; but they managed to convince the congregation the opinions of men was greater and should be obeyed above God's Word.

These spirits told Israel that God led them to Canaan to die; this was because Jehovah wasn't able to keep His Promise. Satan and his demons were dug in deep and only God and His delegated authority could remove them. Moses was God's delegated authority: Israel wasn't a democracy, but a theocracy. Moses could have taken control and ordered the people to possess the land; but for Moses to order scared people to fight would have been a disaster; instead Moses relied upon votes and confirmation. The wealthy place remained with Satan and his wayward children.

A chorus of grief and despair rung through the camp as the heartbroken people wept sorely because they couldn't enter the wealthy place. They cried because they couldn't accept the Word of God; being set in their ways, they believed the words of the ten spies who they knew and saw daily, over God who they barely knew.

Israel wept because the Enemy of their souls told them they were giants and Israel were mere grasshoppers. It was in their own eyes, the ten spies saw themselves as grasshoppers; seeing themselves as grasshoppers, the spies felt unworthy to receive the Blessing and find rest for their tired souls.

If all twelve spies, in unity, saw themselves as more than conquerors, the Canaanites and the unclean spirits would have seen the same thing. The Canaanites would've yielded and given up the land. God's Name would've been honored and reverence.

Joshua and Caleb were types of Christ: Christ had no reservations at being obedient or shedding blood to fulfill the will of God; the willingness to comply and step out by Faith in the Word of God was the key to receiving the Blessing. Where there's no cross, there's no crown.

If the Children of Israel would've "feared not," stood still, like they did at the Red Sea, they would've seen the salvation of God. Instead they took the cowardly way out.

These things were written for out learning; as Christians, we must believe the report of the Lord (that's why we're called Believers). We must name and claim the Blessing and its numerous Promises. As Joshua and Caleb saw the giants as already defeated, we must by Faith view the giants of disease, poverty and despair as defeated foes; we view the giants of addictions, violence and sin as being crucified with Jesus Christ.

Satan and his servants, the giants represent the foul spirits who stole the world from Adam and conspire to keep the material inheritance from Believers. The Word describes us as the head and not the tail; we're lenders and not borrowers; we're blessed and not cursed. We can do all things through Christ who strengthens us, because we're the Righteousness of God in Christ Jesus; a Righteous imputed by Faith.

The giants were men of great statue, serpents in the garden of the Promised Land.

Today, people of great statue with impressive credentials and incredible Hollywood popularity teach philosophies such as **Scientology**, *believe in yourself philosophies*, the **Universe loves you philophies**, **worshiping a higher power**, and the seeking **spirit guides** (which are actually demons) . They believe they can restore, solve the problems facing humanity without the help of God.

They say Christ and the Resurrection Anointing is a myth; and Spiritual Gifts including Healings are past--they only manifested to inaugurate the opening day of the church era; or, even worst, God only heals "certain" people of His choosing; that Christians should be poor, because prosperity is evil, but poverty and humiliated is a virtue. Nonsense. Study the Word and realize the truth.

As the demons "bluffed" Israel and projected a superiority they really didn't have, these same spirits bluff the church of Jesus Christ. They endeavor to keep us looking at ourselves, our past mistakes and failures, what we used to be, sinners. Then the demons rob us blind. The demons want us to view ourselves as sinners, as small, insignificant, weak grasshoppers. Nay, we're more than able to possess the land--and kick some serious demon butt!

Wrong attitudes keep us from the wealthy place of Inheritance. A few of these attitudes are rebellion, religion, doubt, complacency, unbelief, unforgiveness, bitterness, fear, being un-teachable and greed, including the *love* of money (not money itself, but Jesus said, the love of money is the root of all evil; though men have said that it's the "lack of money."

As Israel wandered in the Wilderness of Sin forty years, we too will wander in the wilderness of sin until we make up our mind to believe God and His report over the opinions and theories of man. The witness of God is greater than the witness of man.

Heart check: Do we truly believe that God is able to keep His Promises, defeat our enemies, lead and settle us in the Promised Land?

John the Baptist called the Jewish people of his day a generation of vipers. Today, there are still serpents in our garden, whose intent is to eat up our spiritual progress.

In the Garden of Eden, Adam came face-to-face with the loathsome creature who stole the world from him, and distributed the wealth to his wicked children. We didn't see Satan trick Adam, but believe the testimony of God concerning the matter.

We can readily see the chaos in the world. Like John's assessment, we also live in a wicked, self-serving generation, where evil manifest much quicker than good; (weeds come up when no one actually plants them), where crime and corruption is business as usual, where the wealth of the Children of God is in firmly in the hands of multibillionaires who live for attention, entertainment and sensual pleasures.

Lessons learned from World War I: AI How a defeated Germany rearmed and waged a second World War: Even a defeated foe needs to be watched by the victor lest they rise up and reclaim their territory.

At Calvary, Satan was defeated but still wages war. If we don't keep an eye on his spiritual activities, that is, stay connected with God, the Word, Pray and flow in the Spirit, Satan will regroup, scheme and mercilessly execute future woes and conflicts.

As the Church of Jesus Christ, we're the last line of defense and occupying Christian Army, our orders are to occupy and enforce the victory won at Calvary, until our Commander-in-Chief, Jesus Christ returns.

We war against the visible and invisible schemes; we battle the serpents in our dominion. We often struggle in the world with our walk with the Lord. Yet we keep in mind the Promise of entering into His rest.

We haven't missed the Blessing. Today is a new day loaded to the hilt with fresh manna. We can learn from the mistakes of Israel and not wander in the wilderness, going around and around the same rugged mountain.

The Anointed Word remains as strong as it was the moment God spoke it; this same Word manifests with Power and Glory to change the most ordinary life into the most extraordinary life.

The Word (Christ) didn't profit Israel who heard Him but refused to obey. By hearing the Word, mixing Him with the measure of faith God gave us, put the Word into practice, and the anointing inherited in the Word will detonate and release the Holy Spirit. The Word is alive; the Word is Good News to those who are in bondage.

The fact that others have failed to enter His rest doesn't mean we'll fail to enter in. Faith in the Living Word is the key; Faith is how Jesus Saves.

NEW WINESKINS

After Jesus was consecrated by water baptism, He was immediately Baptized in the Holy Spirit. Then He was driven by the Spirit into the wilderness to be tempted by Satan.

After being freed from Egyptian slavery, Israel was driven into the Wilderness of Sin and temptations; so therefore Jesus was driven into the Wilderness to be tested.

Israel wandered in the Wilderness of Sin and temptations forty years; Jesus lived forty days in the wilderness of temptations. But when the Consecration and Test was fulfilled, He went to a wedding. The wedding was in Cana of Galilee. His mother, who was the host came to Him because she had run out of wine. She was embarrassed for not being able to meet the needs of the guests. She had no husband to turn to; Joseph was dead. All she had was her elder son, who just happened to be the Son of God.

She didn't ask Him to divinely intervene; Jesus could have went to the market and bought wine. Mary trusted His wisdom to solve the crisis without, as mothers often do, tell their child what to do.

She did tell the servants, "Whatever He say unto you, do it" (John 2:5). Jesus told them to bring Him some water pots. The servants brought six water pots full of water that amounted to thirty gallons. At this wedding Jesus performed His first miracle: He turned ordinary water into wine.

So excellent was the wine that Jesus made, the Governor at the wedding called the groom over and complimented him on the wine (the governor didn't know Jesus made the wine).

Most likely, the Governor had attended many celebrations and considered himself a party animal, yet never had the host served the delicious wine last; usually the best wine was served first; after everyone was feeling good or even drunk, the cheap wine was substituted. But at this wedding the last was better than the first!

"Whatever He says unto you, do it," is wisdom of great value to us. As Mary had confidence in the integrity and kindness of Jesus, we must have confidence He's able to handle every situation facing us. He knows the thoughts He has for us and they are more than gracious and wonderful.

Submission to His divine plan is how He solves our problems, as we seek Him in Prayer. Let's not wait until we run out of options before bringing our petitions before the Lord.

The water pots filled with common water symbolizes mankind: We're clay pots filled with the common world. We need Jesus to transform us into a new substance, a new creation.

The new wine represents the Presence and infilling of the Holy Spirit; the effects are the Resurrection of the dead, the Restoration of our spirit, soul, and body. "Therefore, if any man be in Christ, he is a new creature: old things are passed away; behold all things are become new" (2 Corinthians 5:17).

The wineskins Jesus spoke of were goatskins sewed into watertight bags. As wine ferments it produces gas. The expanding gas would split an old, ridged wineskin. So the new wine was poured into the elasticity of new wineskins.

Jesus used ordinary things to explain spiritual truths. The old wineskins were the religious order of His day. The Pharisees strutted about and were strict and ridged; they were quick to point out the sins of others. They were old wineskins that the new wine of the Holy Spirit couldn't occupy for they would burst at the seams. They believed, the old traditions were better. Their traditions made the Word of God of no effect.

The old wineskins are the unsaved and Christians who have become ridged and set in our ways. The Holy Spirit has a mission to change us into the image of the Lord Jesus Christ. Our traditions prevent us from accepting the diversity of ways the Spirit works.

We must change and there's no way around it. The new wine is the new way of living the fullness of the Life of Christ. Our thinking pattern is our worst enemy; our mind needs to be renewed. When the Holy Spirit changes our thinking, then we're transformed from water to wine. The new wine has integrity, character, aroma, power, a sweet-smelling savior.

> "...present your bodies as living sacrifices...And be not conformed to the world, but be transformed by the renewing of your mind," Romans 12:1,2.

If it were impossible to present ourselves to God, lay on the spiritual altar as Living Sacrifices, and afterwards resist the negative aspects of the world, and for the mind to be spiritually and morally renewed, the Holy Spirit wouldn't have guiding the Apostle Paul to write those words; he could have saved the ink for something that was humanly possible.

Can a brain surgeon operate on his own brain and survive the operation? Not hardly; to spiritually change ourselves, our thinking patterns and behaviors after fifty years of sinning. But God through the Holy Spirit can accomplish the task.

Under the Mosiac Covenant, God gave Commandments for the Congregation of Israel to offer various animal sacrifices. These sacrifices were to appease His righteous Justice. Even then, God told them that obedience from the heart was better than sacrifices; and to leave self and idol worship alone.

Under the New Testament Covenant, God won't accept animals but

but a different manner of sacrifice. We're encouraged to forsake our own beaten paths with its fleshly pleasures, and cleave to His paths and heavenly aspirations, to the goal we will know and see the glorious Jesus Christ, the Messiah, the Anointed One.

He wants us to focus our person towards the renewing of our mind and the Gospel of Peace. We're to always be mentally available for the Holy Spirit to restore our soul and renew our mind.

Being a new creation in Christ, the awesome spirit being that we are, God wants only what's best for us; and since He gave His best at Calvary, He expects us to give the first fruits, the best: The unselish sacrifice of self upon the Altar of Obedience, is Holy, acceptable, and our reasonable service.

As we conform to the world we conform to the image of Satan. To love the world is to be the enemy of God. It's impossible for the Holy Spirit to conform us to the image of Jesus Christ when we love the world more and rather than God. Don't be conformed to the world, but be transformed by the renewing of our mind, is what the Gospel states. The renewing of the mind is essential to Sanctification. Once we understand what God's will is, from that moment we should submit to it, and the authority of the Holy Spirit to carry out the Plan, change and bring us into God's perfect will; anything less than submission isn't acceptable.

Christ and the Resurrection Anointing seeks His level in us as we meticulously study and contemplate the Word of God, Pray, Praise and Worship. This provides the correct attitude conductive to the ministering to our mind by the Holy Spirit.

The attendance of Christ-related assemblies, reading Christian books, magazines, watching and listening to Anointed Christian Ministers, tapes and programming helps the mind remain focused on spiritual things; it brings peace to our heart as the Holy Spirit uses these devices to keep us focused and teach us.

As iron sharpens iron, the Spirit teaches us different aspects of the Mystery of Christ within us; he often uses nature to lead us into the profound secrets of life. He revitalizes our worn-out psyche through life experiences, circumstances, conflicts and resolutions with other people. Truly we can work with Him as our Covenant Partner. Serving God is a spiritual and intellectual decision.

Being unequally yoked with unbelievers becomes a spiritual problem. We form relationships wherever we go. At the same time we do not run or hide from unsaved people and hope we can get them Saved, oftentimes that isn't exactly the reason for our relationship; and their reason isn't to serve Christ either.

Toxic Relationships can make our spiritual journey most difficult; coming out from participating in worldly things with unbelievers is expressed in the Lord's words: "Wherefore, come out from among them, and be you separated" (2 Cor.6:17).

Light opposes the darkness and has no fellowship with it; they are two opposites. One of the necessary but difficult Commandments in the New Testament Covenant is the separation from the world.

Denying the self-life is a hard thing; to forsake our worldly associations is equally difficult. Nevertheless, the Word is plain that the unsaved are under the curse of disobedience. If we cling to the cursed, then their curse becomes ours by association; their un-renewed minds and wicked, often blasphemous conversations will poison our mind and bring us back into the captivity of Satan.

On the reverse side, associating with the Blessed will bring the Blessing of the Obedient upon us; the Anointing emanating from them will rub on us; their Christian Conversation will encourage, exhort and lift us closer to Christ.

We had no say at being born into this fallen world. We became a member of a readymade family of relatives and their friends. As we physically and mentally matured, we married and formed our own circle of friends, coworkers and business associates. Now, through the study of the Word we discover that many of these relationships keep us bound to the Law of Sin and Death (because those who are not Born Again are still under the Old Testament, the Law of Moses).

Saved or Unsaved, mankind is subject to the Spiritual Laws; be it the **Law of Moses** (Old Testament) or the **Law Of The Spirit Of Life In Christ Jesus** (New Testament Salvation). No one is excluded, a law unto themselves, but come under one or the other.

Separation and segregation from unbelievers isn't the same thing. We must live and work with unbelievers; we can't segregate and hide from those who haven't accepted Christ. How can we witness to the lost if we-

're hiding from them? How can a doctor in a hospital treat patients if he's afraid to talk or be in the same room with them?

The Word speaks of the *heart separation*, the non-participation and love of sin, the lifestyle, the world system of immorality. The Word of God is that we love the sinners but not the sin; we're in the world but not of it.

The renewing of the mind is an extensive process. What took decades to enslave us won't immediately disappear; and what we never conceived of must be taught or supernaturally imparted by vision or divine revelation.

Salvation, Deliverance, Laying On Of Hands and Healing cleanses us of many demonic yokes--but they're no substitution for the renewing of the mind. We go to one Faith Healer after another to lay hands on us, searching for an easy way to walk the Christian walk. We think if only we'd find the right preacher! Many times the problem isn't demons but our un-renewed mind. And no preacher, no matter how Anointed, can cast out a person's mind!

The separation from the love of the world is a life-long practice but a permanent solution. We shouldn't love what God has separated us from. Faith is believing, trusting in, and relying on God's Word.

There are numerous sins and numerous spirits whose assignments are to empower and endorse them. Hundreds of television shows promote non-biblical behaviors and lifestyles, for example:

> violence, revenge, retaliation, murder, prostitution, homo-sexuality, adultery, fornication, witchcraft, magic, lust, addic-tions, greed, pride, lying, deception, profanity using God or Jesus' Name in vain, and blaspheme.

This type of programming was designed to keep us indoctrinated, in sync and conformed to the world and the ruler of this world.

The Word says, Come out from among them and be separated! We can't allow the television programmers, music industry, U.S. Supreme Court, politicians, abortion and gay rights groups, A.C.L.U. or any organi-zation dictate to the church what we should preach, how we should live, what we should think, feel or wear; neither should we accept as truth the scientific theories regarding evolution over what is written in the Word of the Living God.

The former conversations and nature that feeds the sinful lifestyle the sinful lifestyle must be dealt with; the Anointing, the regeneration power of God must destroy the yoke.

Being a faithful Christian is a process. We have Christ resident within our spirit but our soul and mental facilities, our thoughts are carnal, wicked and our actions traffic iniquity. However, if we purposely flood our psyche daily with the Plans, Purposes and Pursuits of God ---Christ in us---we'll become what we think; we'll become a New Creature in the mental arena. As Covenant Partners, we can assist in our Salvation by, "Casting down imaginations, and every high thing that exalts itself against the knowledge of God, and bringing into captivity every thought to the obedience of Christ" (2 Cor. 10:5).

The old nature is corrupt and can't be trusted; our personality is shattered, fragmented and can't be rehabilitated; it must experience death by crucifixion. We must reckon ourselves as dead to sin, crucified with Christ: "I am crucified with Christ: nevertheless I live; yet not I but Christ lives in me; and the life which I now live in the flesh I live by the Faith of the Son of God, who loved me, and gave Himself for me" (Gal. 2:20).

Our Christian Life truly begins when we die to the old life and become One with Christ. We must daily crucify our sinful desires and thoughts before they become deeds, manifestations of sin. It's easier to live the Christian life if we're not surrounded by unbelief, profanity, perversion, liars and the like.

Often, we have no choice whom we're around; but when we have a choice, choose our Christian brothers and sisters. When we have a choice concerning what entertainment, programming, literature or music for ourselves and family, we should choose Christians-oriented, or at least good moral and family values.

Living a holy life is also a matter of association; whatever environment we feel most comfortable in is the abundance of our heart; out of the abundance of our heart, our mouth speaks.

Now only do we reap what's sown, but we later sow what we previous reaped---whether good or bad--- will receive what's spoken, and eventually become what we think.

Surrendering to the Lord becomes our best option. Then God will keep us in perfect peace whose mind is stayed on Him, because we trust in Him. Only the Spirit of God can impart the truth and change us into the image of the Lord.

22 "But the fruit of the Spirit is love, joy, peace, longsuffering, gentleness, goodness, faith. 23 Meekness, temperance: against such there is no law" Galatians 5:22-23 (KJV).

The Anointed One and the Resurrection Anointing desires to manifest Himself in us as the Fruit of the Spirit; the Fruit of the Spirit is the integrity of Christ; and the integrity of Christ is the character of God. Seeing we have Christ in us Who possesses the fullness and character of the Triune, we must allow Him to live His holy Christian Life through us and with the full cooperation of our mental facilities.

This is the laying aside of the old self--that ridged wineskin--and flex with the gracefulness of the Holy Spirit. His character becomes our character; His Life our life. We know from God's track record that He NEVER FAILS. The Spirit produces in us His traits, Fruit, when we're under His influence. Submission is the way we receive the Fruit of the Spirit.

"THEREFORE BE IMMITATORS OF GOD [copy Him and follow His example], as well-beloved children [imitate their father], And walk in love..." (Ephesians 5:1,2 Amp. Bible). Being an imitator of God is what got Jesus into trouble with the religious order. Nevertheless, we're encouraged to imitate God.

The supernatural things we've read in the Word we're also anointed to do. We give Him the praise and glory for delegating such tremendous authority to His children. The Love, Joy, Peace...we seek from God is already given to us. All we have to do is keep listening to God, get serious about the Christian Life and serve the Lord Jesus Christ. His Blessing will come forth; the power from the highest will overshadow us--and the serpents in our garden will disappear.

We're a living sacrifice; the problem with a living sacrifice is that we keep squirming off the altar! Let's stay on the altar.

RAISING LAZARUS

In Leviticus Chapter Twenty-Five, God gave Israel commandments and ordinances to keep them from oppressing themselves and strangers in their land. God provided a Redemption Plan to protect the poor: "If thy brother be waxen poor, and hath sold away some of his possessions, and if any of his kin come to redeem it, then shall he redeem that which his brother sold" (v.25). 177

To lose some or all of our possessions is a terrible thing, and life would be uncomfortable. In the social circles, sometimes relatives, friends and business associates leave because we would no longer be in their "circle." There would be shame and disgrace. But to lose our personal freedom and become a slave is even worst!

God also provided Israel with a solution to this situation: "And if a sojourner or stranger wax rich by thee, and thy brother that dwells by him wax poor, and SELL HIMSELF UNTO THE STRANGER or sojourner by you, or the stock of the stranger's family: After that he is sold HE MAY BE REDEEMED AGAIN; ONE OF HIS BRETHERN MAY REDEEM HIM" (v.47,48).

Many times in Israel family and friends were also poor so the kinsmen who lost his possessions and personal freedom remained a slave for several years; not being able to redeem themselves and having nothing to bargain with became the plight of many indigent Jews.

God's will for the Children of Israel was to be Blessed: They were to become prosperous owners of land, businesses and international merchants ---lenders not borrowers, free individuals not slaves.

Because of Israel's disobedience, the strangers in their land prospered and many Jews became slaves or servants who dependent on the mercy of their heathen masters.

As a stranger, Satan manipulated his way into the Physical Realm and acquired the inheritance that God gave Adam and his descendents. Satan distributed the majority of this wealth to his servants. He motivates his servants to advance the Kingdom of Darkness and all it stands for.

Satan corrupted the Gory of Man: Man possessed a Wealthy Place of Abundance and Favor. It's Satan who made Israel poor, then they, being desperate and without Faith in God, sold themselves into slavery, hard labor working day and night in the sin mines.

Sin brought sickness, poverty, misery, moral and physical death. But Christ incarnated "to RAISE UP THE NAME OF THE DEAD UPON HIS INHERITANCE ...that the name of the dead be NOT CUT OFF from among his brethren, and from the gate of his place; you are witnesses this day" (Ruth 4:5,10).

We're living witnesses that through Jesus Christ we're not cut off from our wealthy neighbors. Remember, the wealth of the wicked is laid up for the righteous. Jesus is our next of kin--our elder Christian Brother and **Kinsmen Redeemer.** Jesus raised up our names upon the title deed of the Physical Realm; He raised up our names in the areas of spiritual, mental, emotional, physical, and material prosperity.

> 42 "Then they took away the stone from the place where the dead was laid. And Jesus lifted up His eyes, and said, Father, I thank Thee that Thou hast heard Me" John 11:42 (KJV).

Until the stone was taken away, the obstacle standing between the Lord and Lazarus, there could be no miracle, no Resurrection of his diseased dead body. Lazarus was helpless, cold and stiff. Corruption had set in and he stank.

Nevertheless, the Resurrection and the Life came forth and called his name. Lazarus' name was heard not only on Earth but in Sheol. His name was immediately transferred from the book of the dead to the Book of the Living. His name was raised up by the One who had the authority to restore him to his rightful place.

So it is with those who are spiritually dead, whose names aren't written in the Book of the Lamb. Those who aren't Born Again have need to be raised up. Their names require activation as an heir to the riches and Gory.

As a Roman Soldier who had received his orders knew that the orders must be carried out and his own life was expendable--we must accept the Word of God and discard our opinions, by accepting the Word at face value; we must not assume that Salvation and Water Baptism is all there is and wind up severely shortchanged.

We haven't been taught by the traditional church about the depths of the Person of Jesus Christ, His inheritance that we share, nor the power of His Resurrection as He manifests His wealthy Self within Believers.

The Christ in us, the Resurrection Anointing manifests in Believers unto Restoration, Soundness, Wholeness, and Prosperity; this abundance could finance worldwide evangelism.

Satan has never voluntarily give back anything he swindled Adam out of: Finances must be loosed from him in Jesus' Name. Satan uses material wealth to keep the human race bound through regions, philosophies, wars and conflicts, and the love of money; these finances are tied up in non-Christian bank accounts all over the world. Satan's ultiimate plan is to keep these people preoccupied, blinded by riches, fame and popularity, the lifestyles of the rich and famous, until they die. Then Satan has them for eternity and sometimes their parents, and children too.

The departed can't take the riches with them, they are passed down to their children, where Satan does the same thing to them. So for a few billion dollars, Satan directly or indirectly acquires millions of souls. But an individual soul is priceless!

Yet, by the awesome power of the Holy Spirit, these finances are being loosed to Christians: The supernatural transfer of riches and debt cancellation has begun!

> 19 "There was a certain rich man, which was clothed in purple and fine linen, and fared sumptuously every day: 20 And there was a certain beggar named Lazarus, which was laid at his gate, full of sores, 21 And desiring to be fed with the crumbs which fell from the rich man's table: Moreover the dogs came and licked his sores. 22 And it came to pass, that the beggar died, and was carried by the angels into Abraham's bosom: the rich man died, and was buried."

The rich man in this scripture text had it made in life. He lived good, dressed good, ate good, and died good according to worldly standards. In life he was rich; he strutted about the city, an arrogant man, proud and greedy. He cared for his dogs more than the diseased Lazarus who laid at his gate.

Most likely, the rich man had Lazarus run off from in front of his property, but Lazarus always came back. Little did he know, Lazarus was a witness in a divine court case against the rich man; but the rich man didn't know this.

The rich man wished that Lazarus would die, maybe the dogs who licked his sores would infect him, or the rats would bite him. Lazarus was an eyesore; the rich man purposely let Lazarus see his servants feed the dogs choice cuts of meat. The rich man laugh-ed to himself; he had a wicked heart.

The only thing that kept him from getting violent with Lazarus, was what people would think. The rich man was concerned about what the "important" people thought of him; he wanted to please man rather than please God. Lazarus and the rich man died. For Lazarus paradise awaited him, but Satan and Hell awaited the rich man.

The rich man in the above story represents Satan and the unsaved world. The unsaved only entertain and amuse the satanic Kingdom of Darkness. Like Satan, the billionaire in the story got rich by cheating and stepping on others to get to the top of the financial world; he had his fingers deep in the pockets of the community.

Satan has his fingers on the purse strings of every nation. He will always make sure there is enough money to finance his projects. He vigorously promotes his agenda at the expense of those who love God and are temporarily impoverished. We all have noticed how countries always have money to buy expensive weapons to start a war, but never money enough to buy food for its peoples!

The power of the Resurrection is God's righteousness revealed in there being wealth to go around for His people. God showed forth two areas of His Resurrection Power and raised up the names of both Lazarus' upon their inheritance.

The first Lazarus was healed of a terminal illness and raised from physical death. The second Lazarus was resurrected in the Spirit World and experienced Eternal Life. The joy of the Lord became his strength; no more sickness, pain, hunger or poverty for him. He was indeed a wealthy man, for God had made him spiritually rich.

The rich man was materially rich but spiritually poor. Perhaps when he landed he busted Hell wide open!

Christ manifests Himself as Life. The Reconciliation of Christ to Man is the greatest miracle of them all. The Miracles of Deliverance and Healing are only a sample of the power out-flowing from the Lord Jesus Christ. He completes and makes whole everyone and everything He touches.

The Ministry of Reconciliation is in our spirit. The Spirit of God is in us not only to reconcile us, but to reconcile and raise all the Lazarus' who are spiritually dead, stinking, dead men walking in their fine grave-clothes, and living in ten thousand square foot coffins. The ministry to the spiritually dead belongs to Christ. Since Christ isn't the God of the dead but of the living (those in Heaven are considered living too), He Resurrects to newness of Life.

Christ in us to reconcile the lost can't be ignored. The Eternal Christ is the restorer of broken hearts, dreams, the Healer of emotIonal wounds so deep and tender we can't stand anyone else to touch them. Even the thought of someone wanting to know us, befriend us and minister to us makes us want to run and hide!

The Anointed One and the Anointing heals the emotional battle scars of sexual abuse, violence; the hurts of rejection, abandonment, prejudice and racism that left us wounded, paranoid, rejected, with phobias, angry and dysfunctional.

Christ in us reconciles and brings back what the locus, the canker-worm and the palmer worm has eaten up! Even those around us will benefit from the radical change in our attitude and Christian walk.

We may come from a dysfunctional family; but all Human families are dysfunctional! We may have suffered when our parents got divorced; and filled us until we hurt deep inside, even more than we care to admit.

Then our own marriage hit the rocks, our hopes and dreams of love vanished before our eyes. We believed something was wrong with us because we failed to keep our parents together, and now our spouse and children happy; thoughts of inadequacy and depression led us to believe a lot of false things.

Then after reading several relationship books by the "experts," and listening to the daytime Talk Show Hosts, who want people to believe that because they're on television and are known throughout the world, they have all the answers---we come to the conclusion that we're a loser!

But the truth of the matter is: they're indoctrinated, owned by Satan, who financed their affluent lifestyle and placed them in front of the people to give social and moral advice that is contrary to the Holy Bible. One day, if they don't get Saved, they too will land hard in Hell!

At times we want to give up on our child because he or she won't listen to us. Our child has become disobedient and stays in the streets perpetrating every imaginable immoral act and crime. Perhaps they're in trouble with the courts or even incarcerated.

God can raise them up as sure as He raised Jesus Christ! Pray, quote and believe the Word, hold on--because help is on the way! The same God who healed and raised the ordinary people in the Holy Bible will exert His power and restore new life to us, our marriage and children.

It's our mission in life to raise Lazarus. There are billions of Lazarus' on the Earth who need resurrected. They need the Word of Life breathed on them through us. The Gospel of Jesus Christ.

The Great Commission is worldwide evangelism, winning souls to the Kingdom of God. We're created to do the impossible in these perilous times. God has seated us in Christ and put Christ in us.

I AM DETERMINED TO KNOW CHRIST!

The word "know" in biblical sense means a lot more than a casual acquaintance or intellectual knowledge of someone or something. To know, for example in Adam's or Abraham's case, meant to have sexual relations with, to also be legally married to that person.

This relationship is different from the biblical term of "laid with," which implies sexual union without the benefits of marriage, and thus the Blessing of God that accompanies Holy Matrimony isn't present; the latter is sin and a grievous soul-tie.

Therefore to know Christ is more than going to Church, preaching, teaching, singing, ushering, board memberships, tithing and all the other important functions that make up the local churches; but knowing Christ apart from services, programs, duties and people.

Knowing Christ is having intimate, personal contact, a Covenant relationship and open line of communication with Jesus.

We desire to have these lines of communication but someone or something keeps getting in our way. We feel the Power of His Presence while the Praise and Worship music plays, during the Sermon and Prayer Line, but after we leave, it's fades away like the fragrance we put on at 8:00 a.m. but now it's 5:00 p.m. and only a trace remains.

It seems to us that God lives in the brick and mortar building but not in us. Fading Glory isn't what God desires for us; ever-increased Glory is what He wants us to achieve.

Part of the reason that we experience the tremendous Power of God while in the Church building is the Corporate Anointing. Jesus said that where two or three are gathered together in His Name that He would be in the midst of them. It is equally true that an intercessory-prayer-strengthened Corporate Anointing blocks out the overhead Territorial Demonic Powers that interfere in our lives via mental oppression, suggestions and control.

Another reason why we cannot sustain the Presence of Christ in us outside of a Spirit-Filled Service, is the indwelling of demonic spirits in our soul or physical body; these evil entities are silenced, made ineffective while we're in the Presence of Christ and His Anointing, but revive and function when we leave the Church and His Corporate Presence.

Religious Spirits of Tradition, Legalism or Formalism could be present but silenced during the service; they are spirits that deceive us to believe that Sunday Morning Church is good, in that it also makes us look and feel better about ourselves, but it's all that's needed for spiritual maturity, and all t God requires of us as devote Christians. But the rest of the week is ours to live as is good in our own eyes.

Still another reason is that our flesh isn't under the complete control of our Human spirit who is indwelled and being led by the Holy Spirit; there's a part that's too much "us", and not conformed to the image of Christ.

Oftentimes we have a percentage of Christ verses us: 90-10, 70-30, 50-50, 20-80 etc. Once and for all we have to decide who's in control of our life. The lower the percentage of Christ-control in us, the easier it is to return to our old self-life and our scandalous ways.

As Christians we received the Holy Spirit as a complete Person: 100%. We didn't receive a "part" or "piece" of Him; but we do have control over how much He changes us.

In general, sin has a pleasure principle; if every sin brought ex-cruciating pain, no one but the most hard core sadist would have anything to do with it. Our flesh loves to engage in sin; it's comforted and ruled by the pleasure principle. Because sin is pleasurable, the body and mind remembers it so very well, craves it and tries to return to it every chance it gets.

Nevertheless, if we're determined to know Christ in us, there is a lot to overcome in ourselves, our environment and in this world.

God told Jeremiah and it also applies to us: "Call upon Me, and I will answer you" (Jer. 33:3).

In this 21st Century of technology: Satellites, Internet, electronics, Voice Mail and E-Mail, it's relatively easy to contact people providing they want to be contacted. But none of it will help us contact God! He doesn't have a Facebook or Twitter Account, neither does he have a Cell Phone, Laptop or Ipad of any kind.

This is because God communicates at a different level, and has different methods of communication. He often uses the "inner" channel; it's His personal line. Just like the President of the United States doesn't use his personal cell phone or public phone to talk to World Leaders but uses a secured line, a special "Red Phone," so God also prefers this method, so the Devil can't listen in on the call. No credible person ever stated that God calls them on the phone or sends them emails (though we know he can do all these things if He so desires).

Not only can God communicate, but He has promised in His Word to answer us if we by Faith call upon the Name of Jesus. This alone expresses His will towards us: He is able and willing to help! He said, "Ask, and you shall receive, that your joy may be full" (Jn. 16:24).

What we confess with our mouth is also important to what our experience in Christ becomes. The Word in Romans 10:9 says, "If you will confess with your mouth the Lord Jesus, and believe in your heart that God raised Him from the dead, you will be saved."

In the same way that Faith is important to receive Salvation, Faith is equally important to receive Physical Healing or Spiritual Deliverance from the oppression of indwelling evil spirits. A vocal confession establishes in the Earth what is believed [adhered to, trusted in and relied on] in the heart.

There are two biblical Confessions: The Confession of Sin and the Confession of Faith; both are needed to obtain Salvation, and also during the entire Christian journey.

After Salvation, the Confession of sin only applies when we sin after accepting Jesus as Savior and Lord (Jn.3:16). But the Confession of Faith is needed to receive from God what's needed in our life and the lives of others; this includes Deliverance.

It's necessary to pray and speak the Word of God to specifically target indwelling or familiar spirits in our life. Jesus sent His Word to to deliver us from bondage. It is for freedom that Christ has set us free.

Let's look at Joshua and how he obtained the Promise: "Every place where your foot shall step, I have given it to you for an inheritance" (Josh. 1:3).This Word of Promise was given to Joshua and the Children of Israel to stir up their dormant Faith in the God, Jehovah-- whom the majority of the Israelites didn't know, because they were too young to remember the former attempt by their parents to possess the Promised Land.

Their parents, because of their unbelief and a lack of Faith, failed to obtain their inheritance. God was telling this group that Faith is a possessor of the Promises of God, that they should focus their hearts upon Him who is their source, for the battle isn't theirs but the Lord's. God encouraged them; He motivated them to believe His words as though the Promised Land was already theirs----which spiritually (by Faith; the calling things that be not as though they already were) it already was! They were raised up for such a time as this to be conquerors, to take by the force of Faith the Promise that God made.

Even today, we as Christians are to by Faith, take possession of the Promises of God that have been written in the Word of God and purchased by the shed Blood of the Lord Jesus Christ. We are to press in and take what the Word of God generously states belongs to us. By Faith we are to take our Healing, Deliverance, Peace, Joy, Finances, etc., from the clutches and stranglehold of the Devil!

We drive out the evil spirits, the giants occupying e our Promised Land; the "Anakims" of unbelief and fear, spirits who have come between us and our Covenant Rights. And we do not stop until our life and our love ones are completely overtaken by the blessings of God.

> "For we wrestle not against flesh and blood, but against principalities, against powers, against the rulers of the darkness of this world, against spiritual wickedness in the high places" (Ephesians 6:12).

Does every Believer in Jesus Christ need Inner Healing? The answer to that question is Yes! As the above scripture indicates, there is a controlling demonic government reigning and ruling over the

Human population. The descendents of Adam and Eve born into this world are under the curse of the Law (except Jesus of Nazareth). We were born in sin, spiritually dead, and therefore subject to Satan, the ruler (by default) of this world. Everyone, Christian or non-Christian is exposed to the mind control techniques, the controlling and manipulative influence of these Principalities, Powers, Rulers and Princes on a daily basis. These demonic spirits influence and form our thought patterns at an early age; they activate Generational Curses, and thus create mental, emotional and physical bondages, strongholds often before we're born.

In the womb spirits of Rejection and Fear are often imparted by way of the parent's attitude towards the unborn child. Later on, even the best of parents are only Human, impart by way of oral instruction, discipline, lifestyle, or associations their Human wisdom accumulated in and of this world which is demonic and self destructive.

So, it is certain that the worst of parents will impose his or her beliefs, attitudes, prejudices, habits or worldly standards on their children.

Then associations and soul ties at school, frats, lodges, work, sexual relationships (non-marriage), media, music lyrics, and people with toxic personalities add to the already fractured personality; and thus after Salvation Inner Healing and Deliverance is needed. Like old houses, we're all "fixer-uppers."

When we accept Jesus Christ as our personal Lord and Savior, the Holy Spirit indwells our Human spirit and causes us to be spiritually alive. The Presence of the Holy Spirit establishes ownership, and thus the Process of Sanctification commences: We are set apart to serve God; it also includes Inner Healing and Deliverance, to conforms us into the image of Jesus Christ by the renewing of the mind, Healing of Emotional Trauma, instruction in the Word of God, and thus countering the lies imparted and believed this causes the breaking of curses and the ejecting of demonic spirits.

Man has three distinct bodies: A Spirit Body, Soul Body which consist of the Intellect, Emotions, Will, and Imagination (ability to create); and a Physical Body. At the time of Salvation, the Human Spirit Body is indwelled by the Holy Spirit, therefore that part of the Believer is immediately taken care of (Though a person can change their mind and walk away from their Salvation anytime in life there is no "Once Saved, Always Saved.").

Within the last two Bodies of the Believer, Soul Body and Physical Body, Inner Healing and Deliverance is necessary: This is part of the Sanctification process.

The Holy Spirit has to uncover and reveal to us the hidden root causes of stagnation in our spiritual growth, and get our permission and cooperation to resolve it.

This is accomplished by dealing with the mental processes, behaviors, practices, curses, soul ties, emotions, disobedience, parental relationships, sexual sin, strongholds, bondages, addictions and places of frequent visitation have to be addressed and reconciled by way of the cross of Jesus Christ; these things must suffer death, so that the Life of Christ and the effectual power of His Resurrected Life and the Truth will have His way not only where He dwells in the spirit body, but also in the soul and physical body. Then He can bring Healing and Deliverance to the entire Believer; and use that person to touch the lives of others in the Body of Christ and the world.

As Sanctification is a lifelong process, so is Inner Healing and Deliverance. Because the average Christian has experienced many years of "world programming," it doesn't completely disappear in a few minutes or even hours of an Inner Healing and Deliverance Session.

We as Human Beings, like an onion, have accumulated multiple layers of deceptions, illusions, indoctrinations and lies. In the same manner we are instructed to work out our own Salvation, we do the same in our getting set free from the contamination of the world. Believer, don't despair; help is on the way.

May the Blessings of God come upon and overtake you!

The End

www.ingramcontent.com/pod-product-compliance
Lightning Source LLC
LaVergne TN
LVHW021354080426
835508LV00020B/2274